No Place to Land

A Pilot in Coastal Command

J. F. JAWORZYN

WILLIAM KIMBER · LONDON

First published in 1984 by
WILLIAM KIMBER & CO. LIMITED
100 Jermyn Street, London, SW1Y 6EE

© J.F. Jaworzyn, 1984
ISBN 0 7183 0510 8

Typeset by Jubal Multiwrite
and Printed in Great Britain by
Redwood Burn Limited, Trowbridge

Contents

Page

Acknowledgements   9
I   Prologue   11
II   Under Training   22
III   Advanced Training   33
IV   Staff Pilot   49
V   First Steps in the Squadron   67
VI   Over the Bay   80
VII   Last of the Easy Days   99
VIII   Out of my Depth   119
IX   Captain of Crew   128
X   Routine Patrols   145
XI   Facets of War   155
XII   Northern Approaches   170
XIII   Training Again   179
XIV   Epilogue   188
Appendix
       1: The Polish Air Force in Great Britain   195
       2: No 304 (Polish) Squadron   197
       3: Radar in Coastal Command   198
Glossary   199
Index   203

List of Illustrations

Facing page

On board the *Arandora Star*.   16

Arrival: first glimpse.   16

In tents 'somewhere in England'.   16

With Geniek, still in French Air Force uniform.   16

With friends on Blackpool promenade.   17

RAF Weeton in 1940.   17

J.F.J. and Geniek.   17

IFTS. Morse signalling.   32

IFTS, Blackpool 1940/1.   32

With friends at Blackpool, 1940/1.   32

Geniek with friend.   32

Blackpool lodgings.   33

Geniek with his girlfriend.   33

A Miles Magister in flight.   33

Funeral of an air gunner.   48

In Blackpool, soon after obtaining wings.   48

An Oxford in flight.   48

Blackburn Botha.   49

Avro Anson.   49

A group of Polish aircrew.   64

Polish aircrew outside the Blackpool billets. 64

A group of u/t pilots 15 SFTS (P), RAF Newton. 64

J.F.J. at the funeral of a Bomber Command aircrew. 64

Wellington lcs of 311 (Czech) Squadron. 65

The cockpit of a Wellington Mk X. 65

U-boat under attack by RAF aircraft. 112

Wireless operator, E. Siadecki. 112

U-boat on the surface. 112

Navigator, Sergeant Streng. 113

Wellington GR XIVs of 304 (Polish) Squadron, 1945. 113

Before an operational flight. 128

Sergeants Pietraszkiewicz, Wrablewski, Puchlik – 1944. 128

A Wellington Mk XIV at Chivenor. 128

The news of Geniek's death, under his assumed identity. 129

Living quarters on Benbecula. 129

J.F.J. firing a Bren gun at OCTU. 160

J.F.J. at decoration parade OCTU. 160

Interior of a troop-carrying Warwick. 160

Navigator, T. Streng. 161

A Warwick at Chedburgh. 161

Warwick GR. 161

J.F.J. in front of a Halifax. 176

Halifax VIIIc landing. 176

Halifax VIIIc, Transport Command. 176

J.F.J. in 1945. 177

In flight in a Warwick. 177

J.F.J. in late 1945. 177

Acknowledgements

I am particularly grateful to my son Stefan for his invaluable assistance in each stage of the preparation of this book, from typing and correcting the manuscript to acting as my agent.

Many of the photographs were taken by Tadek Streng; I am grateful to him and other former members of the Polish Air Force in Great Britain whom I cannot name, but whose photographs appear in this book.

Thanks are also due to the Imperial War Museum for their kind permission to reproduce some of their photographs.

The appendices were compiled from several sources. I am primarily indebted to Colonel Waclaw Krol's *Polish Squadrons In Great Britain, 1940–1945*, published in Warsaw in 1976.

J.F.J.

CHAPTER ONE

Prologue

5 a.m. 28th June 1940.

The Clyde in thick morning mist. The Cunard liner *Arandora Star* is inching her way into the Glasgow docks. Fog horns bellow, echo off the unseen hills, and are answered by the horns of other ships in the vicinity.

On board the ship are some six thousand troops, mainly Poles, nearly all of them Air Force. This is the last mass evacuation of Allied troops from the Continent of Europe. Dunkirk is long over. France signed the Armistice with the Germans on 22nd June.

*

We had boarded the ship some three days earlier at St Jean de Luz, after a prolonged and exhausting run from the German troops. We had travelled from Le Bruge aerodrome to Dinard some days before. From there we followed a long south-westerly route with stops at all the French coastal harbours. Some of these stops were only of short duration, particularly in places where we saw the ships we were making for burning fiercely, or saw the tops of their funnels awash in the sea. Desperate, we finally made for St Jean, only to find it crowded with troops of all nationalities, cornered in this south-western extremity of France. Spain was but yards away, the border mountains huge and imposing.

I found myself there with a group of Polish student pilots enrolled in the French Air Force. I was then only sixteen years old. Officially, I was eighteen, a plausible age if one is pretending

11

to be one of a group of pilots under training (u/t). The group had coached me in their background, including detailed instructions on how to fly a training aircraft. I had formed a particularly close relationship with Geniek, a small, dark-haired and chunky boy, with whom I shared an almost fanatical desire to fly. This intense wish – almost a physical craving – was shared by all of us in the group.

Now we were trapped in this tiny village, with abundant evidence of the invincibility of the German Army. We were hard-pressed to think of any more places to run to, away from the rapidly approaching Germans. Spain was close by... We tried to think what our chances might be there. Word had soon been passed around (correct for once amid the continuously misleading rumours) that the Spanish were less than happy about welcoming all and sundry into their country. We had in fact seen someone with a badly bruised face, a border stamp we called it, given to him by a Spanish guard who had caught him trying to sneak past.

Where to then? Africa could be reached by a coastal trip taking in Portugal. But we would need a boat for that. Gibraltar? Suddenly a word came up amongst the milling troops ... Britain. Apparently a British ship was coming in. We were doubtful. It was clear that no ship of reasonable size could enter the harbour. Anyway, who wanted to go to Britain? While stationed near Paris we had had brief encounters with the Royal Air Force, mainly the Hurricane squadrons. We could but admire the professionalism of the pilots flying from these poor quality French aerodromes, suitable only for the antiquated French aircraft.

Going to Britain was something else entirely. The islands were so far north, with perennial mists and unending gales; there lived the cold, cheerless, self-controlled British, relatives of the Germans. The Poles, inhabitants of a land-locked country, with centuries of conflict with the encroaching Germans embedded in their national consciousness, were not entirely enthusiastic about the prospects.

However, within an hour thousands of military men filled the harbour, overspilling into the village. A warm summer evening followed the hot day. The crowds milled and stirred, waiting. We also waited.

Around midnight armed Polish Field Police appeared from nowhere. A group of senior officers now stood in the space on the quay cleared for them by the MPs. We were formed into a four man wide snake while the MPs walked through the crowd.

'All Air Force personnel move forward.'

No sooner had the chaos subsided when another order came through.

'Air crew to the front of the queue.'

We shuffled forward again, settled down, smoked, and finally ate the rest of the food we had brought with us. We waited again.

We listened to the rumours. Within an hour word spread around that a ship was approaching. Another hour passed.

'The ship has been attacked by the Luftwaffe. It's been sunk.' That sounded about right. The crowd began to subside. The gamble of waiting for a ship to Britain of all places was too much for many. We stayed.

At around 3 a.m. the MPs returned: 'Back into the queue, identification documents ready.'

One by one we moved forward towards the dark figures. Someone shone a torch on my documents. Someone else asked detailed questions. In many cases they called for witnesses to corroborate identity. It all took many hours. Dawn came, sunrise, daylight. We moved from one part of the harbour to another. Morning passed, the heat of the midday sun demoralised the crowd. Many people left.

The MPs appeared again. Once more the queue. Tired and confused, the soldiers came back with reluctance. We sat in sullen silence.

'We have to leave,' said Geniek. 'This is just another official fiasco.' We decided to wait until midnight.

Midnight. We collected our packs and moved through the crowd. We had decided to make for Spain. Suddenly the crowd surged forward. We heard the noise of motor boats.

'Jesus, we've missed it,' I wailed. We elbowed, pleaded and clawed our way back to the front.

All the quay was full of action now. Fishing boats of all kinds filled the harbour. Within minutes we were being checked and rechecked by the shadowy figures, then directed to the heaving, smelly boats. Outside the harbour in the open sea, a large, dark ship waited. Tense moments of boarding, the precarious jump into space . . . we were aboard.

Well before first light the ship moved off. On board were the remnants of the Polish Air Force in France. Fearfully packed together, we jostled each other for three days and nights, while the ship sailed out of the bay into the Atlantic, finally arriving in the Clyde via western Ireland. Of course, we knew nothing of this at the time. Like most Poles we had never sailed on an ocean, and for the younger of us the trip was like an exciting adventure, rather unreal at times.

*

We disembarked, glad to have this long and cramped journey behind us, and were marched directly to the railway station. We stared in disbelief at the comfortable British passenger coaches. After the French trains we could not believe that we would be allowed to travel in such luxury. The day ended for us in tents, 'somewhere in England' . . . I never found out where.

The summer was sunny and reasonably warm. Still wearing our French uniforms we lounged around, listening to and starting rumours. Unsettled and uncertain of the future we spent the next two or three weeks not really knowing what to expect. Finally we were taken to the RAF station at Weeton, near Preston, a brand new camp still under construction. To us the huts were another luxury. We had not experienced sleeping in a clean and comfortable place since we started our unplanned and unpremeditated journey out of Poland in September 1939, some ten months previously. Now we even had hot showers as well as fresh uniforms which allowed us to delouse ourselves permanently.

Shedding the French uniforms did not involve any nostalgic

regrets. To live in France in early 1940 was to have a few hard lessons driven home to us. Our main preoccupation – a chance to fly – was not within the realities of the contemporary French Air Force. I recall someone commenting to me that at their rate it would take ten or twelve years for our turn to even start training. By that time, he concluded gloomily, we would all be dead of old age or boredom.

Predictably the French went down like skittles once the Germans put the slightest pressure on them. By contrast we ourselves had seen the RAF to be infinitely better organised, equipped and disciplined than the French. But would they be good enough to face the Germans and emerge victorious? All we could do was hope. Now we were in Britain we looked around and wondered. The crowds watching us marching across the towns looked unprepossessing, people of small stature with pale faces, and drab, thin women. And yet they were more responsive than any other people we had come across on our trip from Poland. A few stared at us in silence but many smiled, even clapped and cheered. Considering what a bedraggled lot we had become; hungry, unwashed and dressed in a motley collection of uniforms, the favourable reaction was in itself a wonder.

Soon after the transfer to RAF Weeton came the announcement of the formation of the Polish Forces in Great Britain. An RAF corporal was now in charge of each hut, we were issued with full RAF kits and our pay was increased from 6d to two shillings a day. The plan for pilot training was being implemented immediately. From BBC broadcasts in Polish and our first attempts to read English papers we learned that there was heavy air fighting over southern England, later to become known as the Battle of Britain.

Formal lessons in English were started, and we were assigned to various station duties. The more adventurous of us, but not necessarily those knowing any English, began to go out on short passes. Most seemed to make for Blackpool, the nearest resort, coming back with tales of their encounters with the English.

By that time – August 1940 – most British seaside resorts were no longer open for the usual summer holidays. The few that were

15

became holiday centres for the Northern industrial areas. Blackpool was generally inundated with people from the heavy industry towns of Lancashire and Yorkshire. In addition it was an RAF training centre and a holding unit. Presently it was to accommodate similar arrangements for the Polish Air Force.

However, my desires were thwarted when I fell ill, and for two months could make no attempt to visit Blackpool. Instead I began to visit Preston by myself. If ever a man from Mars has visited earth it is unlikely that he felt less at ease than I did at first. Swamped by the incomprehensible language, the strange traffic rules, difficulties in shopping and in fact by a totally alien way of life I bumbled about, incapable of understanding the simplest signs and signals. Luckily the English seem to come into their own in such circumstances. Having no illusions about the mental capabilities of foreigners they patiently used hand signals and loud monosyllables to repeat instructions many times. Most helpful.

In no time I began to find my way about. Of course all good things have their negative aspects, and ten years later when my foreign accent still provoked the same response I was to be less than enchanted.

More importantly, at this time my claims to be an u/t pilot were beginning to be investigated in more detail. I was growing increasingly anxious; I was supposed to be eighteen years old but I knew I looked like a young sixteen, especially after the wartime diet. Then there was the claim to have been a trainee pilot in Poland. This needed verification, so Geniek spent some time looking for friends who would vouch for me. Once again we spent hours discussing the details of flying training in Poland. Also we had to find a reason why after being born and raised in the south-west I should have attended a pilot school some 330 miles north-east. Still worse was the problem of the medical board: I was not only thin but by the standards of pre-war flying in Poland I was physically not even close to expectations. Absolute perfection in health (which included being barrel-chested) had been the prerequisite for acceptance to any flying school. At that time the Poles had been fanatical about perfection

(...right) On the way to
...in: on board the *Arandora*
...The ship was sunk by
...oats on the next journey.

(...tre right) Arrival: first
...pse.

(...tom right) In tents
...newhere in England'.
...ding on the right: J.F.J.
...Geniek next to him.

(...ow) With Geniek, still in
...ch Air Force uniform.

With friends on Blackpool promenade.

RAF Weeton in 1940. M. Kieltyka on right.

Soon after arrival in Britain J.F.J. and Geniek (first left, kneeling).

in such fields, at least partly influenced by the Germans whose cult of the perfect physique had spread widely. I could expect trouble on that count and both I and Geniek knew it. The only solace came when I found that the British pilots had neither the aspiration nor the need to be exceptionally fit.

So time passed anxiously, although I was to learn over the next few years that waiting for the excitement to begin often entailed a certain amount of boredom.

We sat the preliminary examinations in English and finally visited our 'fellow student pilots' in Blackpool. Less wisely perhaps we also visited the Polish HQ in Blackpool where our young, over-eager faces ill fitted with the rank-studded occupants.

In fact in its initial stages the Polish Air Force in Britain was not representative of its pre-war strength. When the war broke out first line squadrons suffered severe losses and few of their members escaped. The majority of those who did were either from reserve or training units. Thus those who came from Poland were either the older servicemen or the young ones like us. Consequently, as we saw the situation, whenever possible the Poles were bent on reproducing the pre-war organisations and many specifically pre-war military traditions. To us these had become anachronisms, the discredited facets of the old social structure, and thus a source of irritation to a great many of the young Poles about to be trained as aircrew in Britain. Naturally, we would have preferred to operate in the style of the RAF.

There were interminable arguments amongst ourselves while sitting around in the huts about pre-war Poland. Who was to blame for Poland's defeat in September 1939? The sting was partially neutralised by Germany's easy victory over France, but the stand-offish and often arrogant attitude of the French towards those of us who escaped was particularly difficult to forgive and forget. By contrast we found that the British people in the summer of 1940 wore their hearts on their sleeves. The Poles were welcomed by everyone almost everywhere, even though the tales of the supposedly highly-sexed Poles spread around almost instantly. However, in this respect the Poles were no different to the Americans or the Canadians – perhaps homesick men find it

17

easier to lose themselves in the company of women. But we were more than homesick.

For all the superficial flamboyancy, the Poles were worried and anxious – Poland was surrounded in an almost impenetrable fog of uncertainty. When at last news began to reach us the contents were almost too horrifying to be acceptable. The situation began to affect people in different ways. One could spend an evening with someone who would be telling one about his pre-war life with his family, but when the reminiscences reached the summer of 1939 they would suddenly fade, and the speaker would blandly switch to another topic.

Whereas the Polish radio news and the Polish journals published in Britain gave out some information, the English media carried little that would offend a German in his home country. It seemed that Poland might as well be on the moon, and its peculiar inhabitants deserved but passing attention.

Yet for us the news from Poland, scant and impersonal as it was, rapidly exceeded the worst fears which even the most pessimistic of us had expressed. The brutality of the mass executions, the scale of reprisals, the never-ending transportations to the concentration camps . . . all of these became known to us as the war progressed. The Poles and later the Jews issued massive Yellow and Black Books which were circulated among us, and which detailed aspects of life and death under the German occupation. But nobody except us wanted to know.

No doubt during that period I was no different from the others. Silence from my home could mean anything. Unfortunately I was eventually influenced by my friends into sending a message to the Red Cross in Portugal, who issued lists of people looking for their families, irrespective of and without indicating where the enquirer lived at the time. I was uneasy – it all seemed too simple. And unfortunately my forebodings were justified.

The news of my being in the West did reach my parents – via the town Gestapo headquarters. An element of doubt as to the veracity of the information saved my parents from immediate transportation to Auschwitz, located less than twenty miles from my home town. Crippling fines, being placed among the names on the local hostage list, and daily attendance at the Gestapo HQ were the prices my parents paid for my folly.

My diary of 1940 is charged with highly emotional outbursts, and it is difficult to translate the extravagant language of the time. I went through a period of extreme depression and home sickness, and simultaneously went through my first involvement with a girl in Preston. I fell deeply in love with her, though goodness knows how we communicated. I was still not really capable of conducting a simple conversation in English, and perhaps mercifully the affair ended when the girl moved to work in the war industry 'somewhere down south'.

The lesson on my inadequacy in English was not lost on me. However, no such doubts appeared in the minds of my comrades. There was a continuous scramble for postings to Blackpool. Even Geniek preferred a journey to Blackpool than an hour with a book on English idioms.

Finally the day came when I was accepted as a bona fide student pilot. Inevitably the next step was a full medical. Geniek and I travelled to Blackpool for the medical. Within half an hour I was out of the building. The doctors told me that I had a heart problem. I was unfit for flying, indeed for any military duties. A Polish grammar school was being opened in Scotland, one of the doctors told me, and they would see to it that I was accepted there. Dismissed.

Stunned, I saluted and went outside to wait for Geniek.

*

In retrospect it is not difficult to see what happened at the medical. The doctors, middle-aged Polish men, were asked to make a selection of the eighteen to twenty-one year olds applying for aircrew training. Their reaction to an under-nourished seventeen-year-old would have been predictable. Already many people had an idea of the casualty rate among aircrew and the least the doctors could do was prevent a foolhardy youngster from killing himself. As it happened I was extremely nervous and my pulse was very high – a good enough excuse if one is looking for one.

For two days I lived in a complete daze. It seemed impossible that the war might go on and I would not be a fighter pilot, and naturally a hero. Until then I had been convinced that that was how things would turn out. Geniek and I went over the whole topic in detail for two days. At last Geniek had a simple idea – we would swop identities and then follow the established protocol: Geniek would ask for another medical. Having passed far more stringent medicals in Poland and his health being in no doubt he would be bound to pass this one. We would then change identities back, and that would be the last of it.

Changing identities proved to be slightly more complex than anticipated. An identity card in the Forces was the most important document anyone owned. One could not be in any of the Forces for twenty-four hours without having to produce one's ID at least once. We scrutinised our documents in considerable detail . . . our photographs were of course completely different. At least two clear embossed stamps were imprinted on the photographs to prevent what we were about to do: carefully remove them and glue them on the other's document. When we did the results were far from satisfactory – nothing fitted correctly. Finally after another long session we decided that we could not cure, only alleviate the symptoms. We therefore stuck a small cardboard rectangle with our RAF number on under the corner of each photograph. These cards had been given to us for retention in our identity cards because many of us had difficulty in pronouncing our service numbers in English.

Thus I became Eugeniusz Jaworski from Hajnowka in the north-east of Poland, and Geniek became Josef Jaworzyn from Cieszyn in the south-west.

The next step was to tell selected people about our scheme. This we did reluctantly but of necessity because within three days of the medicals we were separated into different units in Blackpool. So I attended the first classes and parades at the Initial Flying Training School (IFTS) under my new name while in a different part of the town Geniek responded to his. He had duly applied for a new medical and had been given a date in three weeks' time. We began to feel uneasy, but presumed that we would be able to sort everything out in due course. Meanwhile I had two parades a day, roll calls during the lectures and various oral examinations.

Three weeks passed and at last Geniek went to his medical . . . and was failed as unfit due to heart trouble. Stunned by this unexpected turn of events we brooded at length over the next step. We could not now change back the identities. If Geniek went back to the training school in my place we would certainly be found out instantly. The punishment for discovery would almost certainly involve the permanent removal of both our names from the pilots' training list. A disciplinary hearing had already removed the name of one unfortunate for the 'trivial' offence of disorderly conduct. Geniek decided that he would stay as ground crew for a while then apply for another medical. Knowing he was fit he felt this would entail only a short delay before he could join me. I accepted his decision with alacrity.

However there were still the twinges of anxiety whenever the ID cards were being examined, which was often. I felt guilty about the problems I had led us both into, and my diary abounds with catalogues of impending doom. Despite the drawbacks I was immensely pleased to have actually made it on the training. I passed all the ground training tests with between 94 and 100% marks and finished first out of 150 u/t pilots on the average marks.

The time eventually arrived when Geniek and I were separated. He was posted to a bomber squadron, RAF Hemswell in Lincolnshire, for general duties. I stayed behind to await a posting to a flying school.

CHAPTER TWO

Under Training

Came the year 1941. Blackpool was full of people, and the crowds seemed worse than ever to us. But then we came from a predominantly agricultural country nearly twice the size of Britain and with only two-thirds of the population. With large parts of the war industry located close to Blackpool it was hardly surprising that the town should be flooded with people.

The town seemed particularly full of girls. Many seemed rather pale and thin to us, and with their small breasts and even smaller bottoms they were not quite the ideal woman to most Poles. They smoked as heavily and drank just as hard as the men, and insisted on paying their share of the expenses. They laughed without inhibition and had an uncomplicated approach to love-making; if they felt like it they did it, inexpertly but with enthusiasm. At least that was the picture we formed of them during their few days' holiday. Coming from their hard war-time working conditions the girls must have found us and the other 'allies' strange and even 'romantic'. It did seem as though the holidays brought out a capacity for intense, if rather short, emotional responses.

Despite the side-tracks we were impatient to be off and flying. We walked along the promenade daily with the crowds, stopping to watch the sea. The sight was novel and strange to us, but we began to learn something of its many moods. We became wary of its fury. Little did I realise how important the sea would soon become in my flying career.

At long last the postings came through. To our great consternation we were not going to flying schools; instead we were being posted to RAF Northolt, more specifically to the 303 (Polish) Fighter Squadron. There was a second Polish squadron at Northolt, the 315, but the 303 was the better known in Britain. To us it was famous, having been the first if not the only Allied squadron to fight in the Battle of Britain, with an impressive score of enemy shot down.

By the time we arrived the Battle of Britain had finished, although the night raids continued with unabated ferocity. The Polish squadrons together with others were engaged in daylight offensive sweeps over France, and as escorts to the Blenheim and Stirling bombers which went out on daylight short distance bombing missions over occupied France.

We were being sent to Northolt on General Duties for a period not to exceed two months. We were to help the ground crews with their innumerable manual tasks requiring minimal supervision by the harassed mechanics. This was one of the rare strokes of imagination from the Air Ministry – sending us out to see the war first hand. We would not arrive at our squadrons in the future with no idea what operational flying entailed.

The first impression I recall was that of how different the people were in the squadrons from those we met in Blackpool: much more direct and helpful, with a clear set of priorities as far as work was concerned. There was discipline to meet the demands, but above all there was a striking atmosphere of tension, of excitement, which gave each day a flavour not easily forgotten.

A good number of pilots had been in front line flying since early on in the war and had by then flown most of the Polish, French and British fighters. Here I was to see that for the fighter pilots there was an element of showmanship, whether in the air or on the ground, which they always retained. In the air they fought – won or lost, lived or died – with others always around them, the ground control always listening to them. Being a fighter pilot at the time was potent stuff, and hardly surprisingly it went to many heads, with some acting out the role that they thought the public expected of them. After all, nothing was too good for the fighters. However, most of the pilots knew that they would enjoy their privileges only as long as they themselves by their skill, cooperation with others and individual luck could stay at their peak each time they flew. One could act, but faking was certainly not possible.

It followed that our six-week stay at Northolt proved to be a memorable one. The sight of twenty-four Spitfires, engines roaring on full power, taking off together and juggling to take up battle stations while climbing towards France followed by the inevitable counting in of the aircraft when they returned is the stuff that films and books thrive on. But the films could not show the looks of the pilots climbing out of their shot up aircraft, their faces flushed with emotions not always betrayed by their voices. And in the moments of waiting for aircraft that would not return the realities of operational flying came home to us.

At Northolt I saw a soldier die in an accident as bizarre as it was tragic. At the time the aerodrome guard duties were still in the hands of the army. One afternoon we watched a Spitfire rapidly taxi towards a patrol crossing the perimeter track. Only when the plane was nearly on top of them did they throw themselves to the ground. A helmet and part of the propeller flew into the air. The Spitfire switched its engine off. A soldier's life ebbed away across the tarmac. An ambulance took his body away. The pilot took off in another plane.

Northolt was the place of my first flights. As I claimed to be an u/t pilot from Poland in common with the others I was assigned to fly a Tiger Moth with one of the squadron pilots. They took their turn with us using the station aircraft. So, one day I was in the plane and was told to take off. I knew from Geniek and his friends about the Polish trainers, but here I had some difficulty in finding the throttle, then in working out that in these aircraft the throttle opened in the opposite direction to those in the Polish planes. Even after that everything went wrong. If one does know enough to push the stick forward for take off, one must also know to pull it back at the correct moment. Then every aircraft tends to swing during take-off and only experience teaches one how to correct for it.

After a struggle between the poor pilot and myself, each fight-

24

ing for possession of the controls, we managed to clear the hangar by inches – or so my friends told me. We were at a 90° angle to the original direction.

'She's all yours,' said the pilot, with nerves of steel. But she was far from mine. We roared and bumped up where we performed turns and duly descended in discreet silence from the pilot.

Near the end of our stay at Northolt we were given our postings; with the exception of two all of us were to go to a Polish training school at Newark. The other two, myself and Kres Gmiter, were to go to the No 4 Elementary Flying Training School (EFTS) in Carlisle. After being kitted out with the u/t pilots' gear we were dropped off at the nearest railway station.

*

Invariably during the war the trains were packed to capacity with the Armed Forces. I was to make many journeys from grimy railway stations where men and women from every branch of the Forces crowded the platforms. One would step over people sleeping, talking, reading or just sitting and waiting. Most carried their kit bags and whatever other possessions they had. The Salvation Army, YMCA and a host of other organisations served mugfuls of hot tea and potted paste sandwiches.

The trains had blackout windows and were packed absolutely tight when they arrived. At night we slept on the floor, in the corridors or in the compartments on the luggage shelves. On the platforms there was an instant and easy informality which often changed to close acquaintance as the journey progressed over the hours. One could meet any number of people, but rarely the same people twice.

Weary but full of high expectations we arrived at Carlisle. We found that we were to be billeted in the town, and hoped that the landladies would be less hard-bitten than those in Blackpool. Generally people proved to be more friendly and forthcoming – with Blackpool being so constantly crowded it was not difficult to see how its inhabitants could become short-tempered.

The RAF station was a great contrast from Northolt. This was primarily a flying school, and no one was allowed to forget it. Discipline came upon us from the first day. Buttons polished, chins up and hair cut we marched around the camp as smartly as any novice from Reading or York, saluting all just in case. Kres had to unlearn most of the rules of Polish military discipline. Even then he thought the rules and regulations almost lax compared with those of the pre-war air force. But when we saw the training aircraft we knew that we were in luck. Ours was the Miles Magister, while most of the EFT Schools flew the Tiger Moth at the time. Undoubtedly the Tiger Moth was fun to fly, but as a preparation for the wartime breed of operational aircraft it was obsolete.

We soon met our flying instructors. Mine was Sergeant H.W. Woodhouse, a tall, brawny man older than most of the other instructors. I learned he had been a teacher in civilian days. Kres and I were separated both in billeting and in instructors. He showed little interest in who his instructor was; having flown before he was full of self-confidence, and the personality of the instructor was hardly likely to have much impact on him.

At last the great day came. Dressed as required by the regulations I was helped into the cockpit, and my straps checked by the Sergeant. I already had an inkling that real flying was not all that easy, that it would require total concentration irrespective of any personal discomfort or distractions, a clear mind, quick and controlled reflexes, and still more. How I would fare, being by nature over-imaginative, nervous and impatient remained to be discovered.

The instructor's voice on the intercom was calm and firm. For some time to come it was the unflappable voice of the sergeant I would rely on. Among the problems and humiliations of the first few days of flying the worst seemed to be taking eight hours before going solo, yet by most standards this was above average. However, obsessed by my own determination to improve I spent hours watching others taking off and landing and listening to the comments of the instructors on their pupils' performances.

Despite my preoccupation with all the aspects of flying, I soon met a girl with whom I was to become very involved. Pauline was a little older than I and about to join the WAAF but at present was still living at home. During my stay at Carlisle we met, with few exceptions, almost every night. I imagine that by then my English had improved or perhaps we did not talk much anyway.

My feelings for Pauline were intense but due to my age fluctuated with the events. That such emotions were mutual one does not necessarily realise at the time. Until one day I was late. We took longer than estimated flying back from a cross-country flight, and at the same time a Magister had crashed in the hills. The rumour that reached Pauline had me in the crash. I arrived to find her in tears, and that evening changed our relationship completely.

Meanwhile I was laboriously learning the rudiments of flying, and in the process learning a great deal about myself – not all of it exactly flattering. The urge to fly at any cost coupled with the real and imagined dangers inherent added to youth's impulsiveness provides a mixture which can be difficult to handle at times. Yet my instructor showed unfailing patience and courtesy at all times. Sergeant Woodhouse, like most of the instructors I came across in the RAF early on in the war, was the embodiment of the dedication and professionalism in the air force. Among the problems which he steered me through was one technical difficulty which was to stay with me in one form or another throughout my flying days. This involved making a smooth three-point landing. I was to learn later that a series of specialised eye exercises might have helped considerably, but this course was not followed at the time. Sergeant Woodhouse, seeing my difficulty, showed me a method of coping with the problem, which involved a two-point landing, which the RAF was accommodating enough to accept. This was simple enough; one in which the aircraft lands on the wheels first and then makes contact with the tail.

Midway through the course Sergeant Woodhouse was commissioned. I was extremely pleased for him, and Kres was convinced that anyone who was teaching me to fly had to have his reward rapidly.

Apart from Kres and myself there was one more Polish student at
Carlisle. He was on a senior course and tended to show it.
Perhaps I was envious of him because he expected and duly
received a posting to fighter training. He was an outspoken and
forceful young man. I was impressed by his intelligence, struck
by the obstinacy of his opinions. We could little imagine what
fate had in store for him: he was to survive the war as a successful
fighter pilot and return to Poland with his English wife and child.
According to the papers he died tragically in the early post-war
years in the town of his birth.

As the course went on we became involved in the various
sporting activities normal in the RAF training schools, which
proved a constant source of comment for Kres. Who needed the
long distance run around the aerodrome, our daily 'must' . . . as
we panted our way around it Kres muttered and cursed, not
exactly looking forward to the afternoon rugby match or the next
morning and outdoor physical training.

When not involved in my romantic evenings, Kres and I went
to the YMCA, a large clean building where the u/t pilots were
identifiable by the white bands on their caps. They congregated
there, and a great many local girls also attended, making it even
more popular. Kres eyed the crowd critically, being highly unim-
pressed by the exhibitionism and posturing of the young men.
Flying was loudly discussed, and often the girls were addressed
in condescending voices, with supercilious smirks. Many u/t
pilots never took their caps off, and these antics proved quite
embarrassing to Kres. We never wore the white bands outside
the RAF station, and when asked what our jobs were in the air
force Kres would answer that we were cooks. I did not entirely
care for that but loyally never admitted to being an u/t pilot
in his presence.

In flying I began to feel as though I were making progress.
Kres acted as an additional stimulant if I needed one, and he
soon led the two of us into highly exciting adventures – low level
aerobatics. First he teased me into a premature attempt at loop-
ing the loop. On a beautiful day while on an innocuous assign-
ment of practising steep turns I climbed to 5,000 feet and

managed the first part of a loop until I reached the upside down position. After that I was totally out of my depth. Suspended upside down I found that my safety belt was insufficiently tight; I was hanging on the belt barely able to reach the control stick, my feet off the rudder and my eyes full of dust because my goggles were off. I could do nothing with the aircraft, which hesitated for a moment then treated me to an upside down flat spin. Having decided I had had enough it gave me another chance by sliding into an ordinary but steep spin. I recovered control at about 500 feet and, shaken, landed immediately. Next time I tightened the belt hard, put my feet firmly into the rudder straps and wore the goggles all the time.

My next step was another type of adventure. Carlisle aerodrome was close to the mountains. I was fascinated. I come from a mountainous region so the first sight of the British hills – desolate bare rocks and wind-swept peaks – made me search for comparisons. Now I was keen to have a closer look. So, having signed out an aircraft for a map-reading exercise, I turned it towards the hills.

That day the clouds were capping the mountain tops, so I flew lower and lower until by the time I reached Derwentwater the clouds had descended to deck level. I tried to fly low over the lake, circling in the clouds which by now were at zero level. At last one valley entrance cleared. I dived for it, not even certain that this was the right exit, and flew low over rocks and farm houses. Suddenly I was out. I recounted this private piece of tomfoolery to no one on my return.

However, the games Kres and I began to play were far wilder, pushing me well past any limits of caution I would have marked out for myself. Kres was of course well ahead of me in controlling the aircraft.

'Did you do the aerobatics today?' he asked me one day.

'Of course I did.' I was by then authorised to carry out various manoeuvres at about 3,000 feet.

'How long does it take you to climb to the starting height?' He knew full well that out of an hour flying time I would spend more than twenty minutes climbing back to the required height for the aerobatics. Having thus needled me he explained the basis of his approach: it was simple – start all your aerobatics at less than 2,000 feet. But . . . but one was supposed to finish at 3,000 feet, I argued. After all, there were the loops and slow rolls for which the Magister's little engine was no help in maintaining and controlling the level of the flight. Kres shrugged and pulled a face. He would arrange to go solo at the same time as I did, he said.

I had the first inkling of his presence when a Magister dived at me, passing but feet away before falling away in a dive. At about 1,000 feet he pulled the aircraft into a loop. The next thing he was in close formation with me. This was real flying . . . He urged me on, and at 1,500 feet I pushed the aircraft into a dive. From now on I would stop looking at the altimeter at all times, I resolved.

The rest of the hour was nothing I had experienced before – we looped the loop lower and lower and fought wild dog-fights right down to ground level. I landed feeling a few inches taller. Heights, speeds and regulations were, as I had always suspected, for simpletons. My hands shook with excitement. I chain-smoked. Kres gave no indication he had noticed. He went over the manoeuvres of the day in detail, pointing out the mistakes I had made at various points. No doubt I flew better next time but was hardly likely to match him in his skill and daring.

Inevitably I came to situations where the engine stopped while I was throwing the aircraft about at extremely low levels; then in silence, with seconds left I would search the ground for a place to land, at the same time following the drill Sergeant Woodhouse had taught me for such occasions.

The end of the course was approaching rapidly. We left no stone unturned in our efforts to impress our instructors that we would make the best candidates for fighter pilots. I learned even more frenetic aerobatics until I could make the whole landing circuit flying upside down. I would turn the aircraft in a side-slip simultaneously lowering the flaps. . .

Throughout all this Woodhouse behaved impeccably. After all, a lot of our antics went on very close to the aerodrome. No one could have survived a week as a flying instructor if he were not observant enough to see what was going on. Nevertheless he made no mention of any untoward activities. After each landing we would sit down and systematically discuss how to perform a steep turn without losing or gaining any height.

Three days before the end of the course both Kres and I were given the times for our final tests. We decided to have one last fling and chose lunchtime when few instructors would be around. We had only just taken off in a spectacularly tight forma- tion when Kres's aircraft suddenly disappeared. Instead another Magister was now close to mine, and someone in the instructor's seat kept pointing down. Suddenly I knew. The white overalls were those of the Chief Instructor, who was of course taking the final tests throughout the lunch-time also. I landed.

Nothing was said to us. In the afternoon Pilot Officer Woodhouse and Kres's instructor, spruced up in their best blues, made their way towards the HQ. Only then did I have a brief and inconclusive interview with the Flight Commander. He was not interested in any details, he said. It was altogether out of his hands.

Much later Pilot Officer Woodhouse called me in. He looked grim and my heart sank.

'You've had your flying . . . here,' he said. 'You're suspended until the end of the course.'

'And my Final Test?' I knew that one could not be passed out of any Flying School without such a test.

'Under the circumstances surely not having one is an advan- tage?'

By this he saved my skin . . . the Final Test could have been carried out by the Chief Instructor.

I did pass out of the school, but was graded as 'average'. I was an ungrateful, callow youth, and having been passed out as only average I felt very bitter. I was ten times as good as the plodders around me, I complained to Kres, who, in such situations pre- ferred to take a lofty 'do not bother me with the trivialities of life' attitude.

The last few evenings were very difficult. Pauline and I had grown very fond of each other. I was upset at her tears. Since I had left Poland only Geniek had taken an important place in my affections, but now Pauline had too.

(*Top left*) IFTS. Morse signalling using Aldis lamps, on Blackpool sands.

(*Centre left*) IFTS, Blackpool 1940/1.

(*Bottom left*) With friends at Blackpool, 1940/1.

(*Below*) Geniek with friend on Blackpool pier.

Aircrew relaxing.

Geniek with his girlfriend.

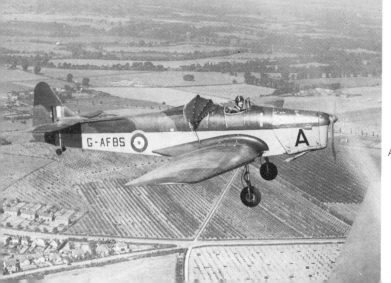

A Miles Magister in flight.

CHAPTER THREE

Advanced Training

From Carlisle Kres and I made our way to a holding station in London to wait for the Air Ministry's orders on our next posting. A fairly large group of Polish u/t pilots was already there. It was early 1941, and the air raids on London continued. The major feature of the air war at the time was the lengthy and intensive night bombing by the Luftwaffe.

We had seen the Luftwaffe in action in both Poland and France, almost always in daylight raids. There the air raids seemed a more intense and personal experience, a more direct threat. A different impression was gained while in London during the raids. The intensity of the anti-aircraft fire, the searchlights, the balloon barrages – here the British were fighting back, doggedly, whether effectively or not. The Luftwaffe could not have its way, could not destroy the city quickly, but had to try to wear it down by repeated bombing. But no matter how abysmal the picture of destruction looked the English were not to be worn down, as we by then understood. So one found out which part of the city was being bombed that night and then proceeded with one's business.

In London I met Geniek briefly. After making a nuisance of himself his superiors conceded to yet another medical, which was coming in a couple of weeks. Geniek had matured with his difficulties. He was not entirely pleased with me. Taking risks in flying he could understand, but risking a career through stupidity was definitely not his idea of intelligent behaviour.

At last the forty or so of us were paraded, and the CO came out holding the orders. When he began with, 'The Air Ministry postings are decided primarily on the basis of the urgency of the current need for pilots . . .' I knew that I was not going to be too pleased with what followed. One person went to the fighter Service Flying Training School (SFTS), thirty-three, including Kres and myself, went to the twin-engine SFTS at South Cerney, and the remainder to the Polish No 15 SFTS at RAF Newton.

The idea of being a bomber pilot had never entered my head; in our terminology a bomber was a flying cow. Accordingly we paid little attention to the bomber aircrew for 'this could not happen to us'. The nightly slow plod to and from Germany in the ungainly cows was the antithesis of the freedom of the blue sky and the swift, elegant manoeuvres of the Spitfire. It looked as if the idyllic days of our flying adolescence were over.

RAF South Cerney was a peacetime aerodrome. Two-storey living quarters surrounded the parade ground. The grass aerodrome was large, and the hangars matched the rest in their size and solid construction. The air was very busy. Twin-engined yellow trainers – 'Oxfords' – abounded on ground and in the air. Our hair was shorn extremely short. Discipline was strict, the airmen fell into twos and marched stiffly around.

Our class was a large, mixed Anglo/Polish one, the emphasis being on cooperation and equality of treatment. There was a whole range of military ranks, as well as ages, from seventeen like myself to thirty-two, the upper limit at the time. Since we all lived together we examined each other with curiosity. One way or another not all of us would cope, but who and why? Would it be the emotional Poles, or the cautious, disciplined English, whose initial reasons for volunteering to fly often had an entirely different rationale than ours.

There was no doubt that the English pupils were very keen to be seen doing the right things, and their zeal seemed a little misplaced until we discovered that commissions would follow for the right people. That did not apply to the Polish u/t pilots, which emphasised the difference in attitude which emerged during the training.

We soon settled into the busy daily routine. The major problem was that as our windows faced the parade ground, it took some time to adjust to having the Station band practising in front of us most mornings. Commendable as it was, since it coincided with our breakfast time, we were rather puzzled by the choice of tune and its constant repetition – it was Chopin's 'Funeral March' . . .

With another Pole and two English students I was assigned to an instructor who was very different to old Woodhouse. He was Pilot Officer Frith, young and fair-complexioned, faultlessly dressed and spoken; altogether 100% in efficiency and enthusiasm. Frith's qualities as an instructor were superb, and I can but repeat my unqualified praise of the English in their flair for instructing and training, particularly in complex and hazardous areas such as wartime flying.

It was well I continued to be lucky with my instructors. My first attempts on the Oxfords were dismal. I was overwhelmed by the complexity of the controls and instruments, and the manipula-tive skill required to fly a twin-engined aircraft. Even Kres found it tricky to control: it was basically underpowered, as was the case with many RAF aircraft of the time, and unforgiving of errors, particularly at low speeds. The regular practice of the Chopin march was a good reminder of this.

But Pilot Officer Frith was not a zealous instructor for nothing. His pupils had to be the best. Within three days of the first familiarisation flight, I went solo, the first in the whole Anglo/Polish course to do so. Short lessons in map-reading were given, and after that the pupils went out and did the best they could.

The experience was terrifying; the dual controls mimicked my every move. As I accelerated over the bumpy ground my mind repeated Frith's instructions as though I were listening to a tape recording: 'Keep her straight, straight, watch that starboard wing, rudder, more rudder, speed, up now, speed, on course, horizon, speed.' And so on, step by step, to the final turn, the decision of when and where to execute the various stages of the landing procedure.

So I was off and flying. Others followed, except for two English students who could not solo within the allotted time. We flew a

35

great deal that early summer, perhaps four or five flights a day, rapidly absorbing as much as we could in such a short time. We soon began to know one another.

For a time I flew with a Polish pre-war pilot who was very formal but an excellent, clear-minded pilot, in control both on and off the ground. I learned a great deal from him, but I doubt whether the experience was mutual. I was lucky enough to begin my cross-country flights with him, for we had to fly under weather conditions no civilian pilot would find acceptable: 10/10 clouds, mist, base below five hundred feet and no radio. It would have been more than I was initially capable of by myself, yet he saw us through.

The school could not afford to be fussy about the weather they sent us out in, because one could be sent directly from the SFTS to an Operational Training Unit (OTU) to fly in operational aircraft with full crews.

The problems of cross-country flying were manifold. Apart from the often poor weather conditions, the countryside itself was not that easy to unravel on the maps either. All identification markings were removed from the aerodromes, railway stations and even cross-roads. Fields were covered with anti-landing devices and obstructions. The railway system of the day was complex and extensive, while narrow insubstantial country roads meandered in great profusion. Throughout the war radio masts were being put up by the dozen, and huge industrial towns belched forth smoke and fog across large areas of the country. Add to this the forbidden zones, where any aircraft could be shot down, and the barrage balloon cover and the results could often be disastrous. We found it hard going, but when fully trained aircrew from the Commonwealth centres in Canada and South Africa began to arrive, their elementary airmanship blunders led to the countryside, and the hills in particular being full of aircraft wrecks of all shapes and sizes. Many of these still remain as a tragic testament to the dangers and difficulties of wartime flying.

Cross-country flying had to be learned from experience, often dangerously. There was simply not enough time to teach everything.

My first hard lessons came when I started flying with a different pilot, and we ran through many variations on the above problems at the time.

I soon learned that there were other frustrated fighter pilots amongst the Polish pupils besides Kres and myself. They also felt victims of the system, and thus entitled to something better than instrument flying or criss-crossing the countryside. Kres became the leader, and he soon established the low-flying craze, having discovered that the Oxfords were somewhat clumsy in aerobatics. However, the excellent visibility of the aircraft and the quick response of the controls made it particularly suitable for very low level passes over unfortunate farmhouses. Kres, having sweet-talked some Land Army girls, would mark up on the map places which he then allocated to each of us. Although at that stage I was not so hooked on low flying, I followed the lead of the others, and we duly made a nuisance of ourselves.

Kres meanwhile had grown bored with low flying, and went back to trying a few tricks. He finally settled on one particularly hairy manoeuvre; he did the first part of a loop, then, while climbing very steeply on full power suddenly closed one engine. The aircraft turned like a spurred horse. He did not elaborate on what a risky stunt this one was. One miscalculation would lead to a nasty form of spin, with no chance of recovery.

I tried the stall turn. During the first attempt the aircraft juddered, side-slipped crazily, stalled and began to spin. All I could do was pull her out, losing 3,000 feet in height in the process. I did not like it; the Carlisle confrontation was still clearly in my mind. Also, while Kres dominated the aircraft, making it work as he wanted it to, I did not have the physical stamina nor the will for this approach to flying. I preferred to learn how the aircraft handled and then exercise control over it. In fact, someone later commented that you don't fly the aircraft, it flies you . . . well, perhaps we compromised.

*

The Clifton suspension bridge in Bristol is of course a well-known landmark, and it seemed inevitable that we should discuss it one evening. Staszek and his friend Zenek said that they would have a go at flying under it. Only one voice rose in protest, that of a young university student named Rysiek. The rest of us shifted about uneasily but said nothing. I had taken a look at it myself without telling anyone, and at that stage of the training the bridge looked diabolical to me: the gorge would be full of unpredictable air currents and the approach very tricky. The various obstructions would need to be carefully investigated before any attempts were made to fly under it.

According to the records, Staszek and Zenek took off the next day for sixty minutes of instrument flying practice. The time was 10.30 a.m. By lunch-time their bodies were in an ambulance on their way back to the aerodrome. They made it under the bridge, but hit the trees immediately afterwards. In the excitement of the moment they did not seem to have allowed for their presence.

When the band practised Chopin the next morning, we lay awake in silence. The funeral took place the following day. I was one of the bearers.

*

The same afternoon as the funeral we were back to flying. More lectures on theory and a series of written examinations. Rysiek came first in the class, and a clean-cut English student second. I was only third this time. Soon after I made myself a closer companion to Rysiek. No doubt there was an element of opportunism in it, yet there was another reason – I simply liked his company. He was a cheerful, healthy extrovert, tall with fair curly hair and a smile marked by a gold crown on his front tooth. Very rarely did he have a harsh word to say about anyone, a great contrast from myself. He was deeply religious without being ostentatious, and had a natural, easy charm.

Rysiek and I teamed up for the last and longest cross-country flight of the course. Our route took us across to the east coast and back – without landing of course. We made it exactly on our Estimated Time of Arrival (ETA), and on submitting our flight logs were given an 'excellent' mark.

In the meantime I had applied for four days' leave, and much to my surprise had it granted. I went to see Pauline, now due to leave for the WAAFs any day. I had been writing to her frequently, and had hardly gone out to Cirencester, the nearest town, although the pace of training was enough in itself to keep one close to the base.

With the deaths of Staszek and Zenek we began to experience a growing isolation from the people beyond the boundaries of the aerodrome. It was hard enough to communicate in English, impossible to convey the significance of being Polish under the current circumstances, and now with flying taking on a new aspect, what was there to say that anyone would be interested in unless he was personally involved? It was not the fear of death which was worrying me but rather its inevitability that began to dawn on me. But whose death? Certainly anyone close to me and involved in flying. And what of me? I would keep on flying, I knew that, but only an optimistic fool would think further ahead than the plan for the next flight.

Of course I had not forgotten about Geniek. We corresponded regularly, and were going to see each other at the next opportunity. He had been given a date for his latest medical which would almost coincide with my half-term pass. He preferred us to meet later on as he was becoming rather nervous concerning the whole issue.

In June 1941 an event occurred which was to have a profound effect upon all of us – the invasion of the USSR by the Germans. The entry into the war by the Russians seemed to have an enormous impact on the British. All things Russian were instantly at the top of the popularity list, and coincidentally the Poles appeared to sink almost to the bottom – a position we were to maintain for the foreseeable future.

On one of my infrequent visits to Cirencester I noticed that some of the Polish pupils had been drawn into a rather heated political discussion. Emotions became hard to control, but whereas in Blackpool a fist fight would almost certainly have ensued, our pilots here behaved differently – they simply ceased taking passes out to the town.

It is pertinent that as the war progressed the Poles did become more 'controversial', until by 1943 they were classified as rock bottom in popularity on a par with the American GIs – even below German and Italian prisoners of war. Those who garnered the most interest and sympathy were the Dutch and the Czecho-slovakians; the Dutch had their ever-popular Queen Wilhelmina in exile, while the whole Western world talked of Lidice . . . Hollywood made a film about Lidice, a Czech village destroyed with its inhabitants by the Germans, in reprisal for the assassina-tion of Reinhard Heydrich, deputy leader of the SS under Himmler. However, there was a Lidice in Poland almost every week.

Before I took my leave I had yet another first – an introduction to night flying. This was hardly a 'Sand, Wind and Stars' epic, but an almost desperately difficult start to what is not the easiest task even at the best of times. To me night flying became another watershed, a further element in the natural selection process – if I could come out of this unscathed it would certainly be a step in the right direction.

At the time Britain was at the peak of the Luftwaffe raids. Extreme precautions were taken everywhere. For night flying we were transferred to a small satellite aerodrome, where the entirety of the night flying illumination consisted of a single line of hurricane lamps, a glide path indicator and a yellow low angle beacon located between three and six miles from the aerodrome, the location of which and its signal were changed nightly. Com-bined with a total blackout, and a dark, moonless night, the scene was set for my first night flight.

But Frith, newly promoted to Flying Officer, was not to be dis-couraged. He obviously knew what my capabilities were, or he would not have taken the risk of sending me up. Even though I knew the whole cockpit layout and flying drill by heart, I still managed to stumble into the aircraft, hitting myself on all kinds of protrusions in the darkness. At last we settled down to inspect what was visible inside the aircraft; two tiny lights just illuminated the instrument panel.

The sequence was to be as follows: Frith would first fly the circuit himself, talking his way through the drill. We would then fly it together on the second circuit, and finally I would make a solo attempt, but with Frith remaining in the aircraft 'just in case'.

The first time around I sat in petrified silence. This simply could not be real. The take-off on the bumpy field with the few lights speeding past us was a nightmare, but worse was to come – once we pulled off the ground there was total darkness outside, and any air disturbance made the instrument needles jiggle and jump madly. There was the comforting sound of the engines roaring steadily though.

For acclimatisation Frith took the aircraft up to 1,500 feet and circled for a few minutes, then we went through the landing drill and a descent down the glide path. Gradually he shut the engines down until there was only a swishing noise with no visibility at all. At last we hit the ground, and bumped our way along the line of lamps.

The second circuit passed uneventfully, apart from the bone-shaking landing, and then we were off again, with me at the controls and Frith nagging at me from the darkness. When I finally bang-crashed the aircraft down onto the hard ground I was shattered. I had had enough. Nobody could be expected to master this travesty of flying . . . We taxied back to the take-off point in silence, with me feeling quite sorry for myself.

There was some commotion on Frith's side, and the next thing I knew he was out of his seat.

'All right, Mr Jaworski, she's all yours. Off you go. Don't worry – just remember the moves.'

Surely he was not going, would not dare to leave me on my own here? He went. The door slammed shut, the green light flashed, and I was away.

The throttles were fully open, and I was soon bouncing along, the aircraft roaring away and trying the usual trick of swinging itself off to starboard. Then there was the darkness again, and except for the speedometer none of the instruments registering any worthwhile information. In these few critical moments one simply had to learn and master from experience. The aircraft was soon flying well, and except for some panic on the final approach where the aircraft had to match correct safe descending speed everything seemed to work out. Came the dreaded moment, I closed the engines. The ground was there somewhere – just how close I could not tell. A sickening thud and a bump and I was down, but not quite. Another bump. All I could do was keep the aircraft in line until it bumped itself out like a truculent goat.

I was glad to be out of the darkness when the instructor appeared.

'Congratulations, Mr Jaworski,' he said in a brisk manner. 'You are now qualified to fly at night.' I sat in disbelieving silence.

Soloing on the Oxfords at night after one hour of flying was not to be achieved by anyone else on the course. Even though I had a feeling that I had been tricked into the performance, I would in due course witness some appalling examples of bad to disastrous night landings. I came to realise that the instructors, many of whom, not surprisingly, disliked the dual night flying, needed the psychological boost of an early breakthrough with a night solo on each course.

A few days later I was on my way to Carlisle. I hardly noticed the journey, my mind wandering into a state of half dream, half nightmare. Thoughts of flying crowded my mind, particularly night flying. I started thinking about how useless the link trainer, a mock-up aeroplane with a well instrumented panel, was in the context of night flight.

I remembered one episode where I had become so enraged by the insistent correcting of a keen young WAAF officer that I let the trainer fall into a spin and sat there, not touching the controls, whirling around crazily until she stopped it and let me out. We stood and glared silently at one another. She knew that to challenge a foreigner over disobedience of this kind would be no easy matter; after all, who could tell just how much they understood of what was told to them? In fact, who could tell whether they could comprehend anything at all?

Of course young Frith was informed, but even he balked, and

led away into a generalised chat on the importance of trying to apply oneself to the link trainer practice. Of course, I had realised that in real night flying one could not stop the difficulties by a temperamental display and then step out into the darkness intact.

Still preoccupied, I arrived in Carlisle to be met at the station by Pauline, looking neat, tidy and as lovely as ever. I stayed at her home, situated out of the town in the quiet countryside. Although the wartime rationing and regulations had restricted the family style, it was still considerable and impressive.

She and I went for long walks in the country, trying to ignore the topic of flying and the aircraft which droned ceaselessly in the background. There were Magisters, Spitfires and Wellingtons all stationed in the vicinity. Somehow we managed to avoid the issue . . . But all too soon I had to be off again. Pauline was also leaving, in ten days' time.

She cried at the railway station, and I shifted about uneasily, torn by my desire for her, the sorrow of the parting, and a wish that the train would start and end the upsetting situation. Then I was back in the corridors of the packed wartime trains, engines wearily puffing out clouds of steam, smoke and soot, distributing the grime evenly on the countryside and us. That summer was especially warm, and we squatted in the corridors, crammed like sardines and sweating profusely.

Next morning I woke up in my bed at the RAF station once again to the tune of Chopin's 'Funeral March'. 'Time for breakfast,' some callous young soul would shout. It was good to be back. While on parade that morning we discovered that one of the Polish officers had decided to leave and go back into the army. We were sorry about it. To us it was understandable if any of the English pupils were to decide not to continue, but until then I doubt if any of us had considered that he may not learn to fly.

'Good leave, Mr Jaworski?' Frith eyed me with an amused expression when I pretended I had more to hide than I actually did. This came from the worldly 22-year-old, speaking to a

Polish u/t pilot who was not yet even eighteen.

'Oh yes, fine, sir.'

'Good, good. Off you go then for an hour of take-off and land-ings,' he said with a hint of malice. I hated them, and we both knew it. Endless circuits, with long lines of aircraft taxiing towards the take-off point, an over-crowded sky. An overspill aerodrome took away some of the excess traffic, but the air was still swarming with Oxfords circling this way and that. One had to be on one's toes, so to speak, for most of the aircraft were flown by fairly inexperienced pupils who had been sent out on a variety of tasks.

I was queueing for my third take-off, idly watching the aircraft coming in, evaluating their techniques. Suddenly I caught sight of an aircraft banking in a descending turn for the final approach, then apparently stopping in the air and at once plung-ing to the ground in a half spin. The noise of my engines drowned out all external sounds. There were no smoke, no blaze. Almost at once I was given the green light.

I checked my cockpit meticulously, my mind working furiously to cancel that unacceptable snap-shot view. The port engine was dropping revs on full power. I could have turned back and grounded the aircraft. But not this time. I was covered with sweat before the aircraft left the runway, my legs shook from the effort of keeping it on course. Once up, I found that the wind was strong and blustery. I glanced down at the mangled remains of the crashed plane, and saw the ambulances clustered around the wreck. I kept myself busy flying.

On returning to the flight office I discovered that it was one of ours – an English u/t pilot; but we would not be going to his funeral. The English had their own family funerals, which we rarely, if ever, attended. We commiserated amongst ourselves.

Presently we moved on to more complex flying – instrument flying, followed by elementary formation exercises, where we all found that the twin-engined aircraft required more practice and concentration than the single-engined ones. Unsurprisingly the instructors were slow to let us go on solo formation flying.

Meanwhile Frith flew less, since he now began to assist the

Flight Commander with his administrative tasks. I was parcelled out to a variety of different instructors. I rather enjoyed it, even though I suspected that Frith was doing it because he knew that one of his pupils could smugly carry out any of the complicated manoeuvres required, while the other students had to sit and watch. I also went up frequently with the Flight Commander. I am not so certain I was liked by all the pupils. . .

Where I was still reduced to struggling like the others was in cross-country flying. The statutory requirement was the completion of five cross-country flights, actually ten, because each flight had to be flown as a pilot and as a navigator. Bad weather, getting lost or any other problem could, and did, curtail the flight, in which case one had to repeat it over and over again.

Before going on the dual cross-country flight it was necessary to do a single half hour solo. Most of us performed this early on in the course. Inexplicably one of our Polish students, a quiet and unassuming boy named Grunecki, had a solo cross-country left over. He set off one day in the early morning, and had not returned by lunch-time. He was brought back the following day in a coffin. He had been collected from a small peak close to Gloucester. Thus we marched the funeral march again.

We restarted the night flying. To my horror I realised that Frith had had me solo night flying some six weeks before the rest of the course had even started duals, and now I would have to wait for the others to catch up. I needed to practise night circuits and bumps, but for night flying we needed a co-pilot to be present at all times.

On my first doubles I went up with a Polish corporal who experienced difficulty in keeping up even in the daytime. The night of our flight the weather was poor, the cloud ceiling steadily lowering. We realised this because the beacon flashing the letter of the night, which until then had been our major source of direction finding as well as making us feel slightly more secure, could only be seen intermittently.

I was flying first. In the absence of instructions to the contrary we plodded grimly on, swopping seats after an hour. I sat morosely watching his antics. Naturally I thought he was terrible, his ropey low-speed landings and homicidal take-offs. After his second take-off we saw nothing outside in spite of the regulation turns.

'We're in the clouds,' I said at last. He began to lose height, flying in who knew what direction. 1,000, 900, 800, 700 feet.

'Turn,' I shouted out, infuriated and anxious. He turned. We had momentary glimpses of lights below us, coming at all angles and disappearing in the darkness.

'Lower.'

At 500 feet he did a series of steep turns, trying to line up onto the flare path. Now totally confused and bewildered, he made a mess of the landing drill, and came in at an angle to the flare path.

'Land,' I shouted. I was certain that from now things could only get worse. He landed smoothly, and we bumped our way across the flare path and into the hedge.

No harm was done to the plane. We found out that all flying had been stopped some time earlier due to cross-winds, rain and a cloud ceiling which at times had been below 100 feet.

It took a few days before the corporal and I spoke to one another again.

*

The course was nearing its end, and none too soon. There was too much to learn in too short a time, little room for error, no allowances for the impulses of youth, no room for posturing. As the final test was approaching, we were sent out for an hour at a time to practise the most likely of the difficult manoeuvres we may have to demonstrate. Once again I paired up with Kres.

He had not really settled down; his aerobatics were even more breath-taking in their audacity and complexity. He roared up and down and sideways around the sky. That kind of flying was well above my head. I just held on like a terrified cat while we dived and flew through the valleys, passing close to the farmers' windows, roaring up in steep and controlled turns. Kres was a master of his craft.

The day of the final test came. We were approached by Sergeant Steel, Kres's instructor.

'One of you comes with me for the final test, the other can go up for an hour to practise steep and climbing turns. Sort it out between yourselves.'

I would rather have taken the test after Kres; I was slightly nervous, and I had promised a girl in the Land Army that I would do some low flying over the farm where she worked.

We tossed and I lost. I threw my flying gloves at Kres, and he laughed. I left with Sergeant Steel.

We were about halfway through the flight when Steel said, 'I'll take over.' He was looking at something on the ground, a small circle of burned out grass. There was debris scattered around the field. We cut the flight short and returned to base.

Steel was out of the aircraft and running for the Flight Office as soon as he had switched off the engines. Steel came out of the Flight Office with a peculiar look on his face. He grabbed my arm. I went through a trauma, a momentary emotional paralysis.

'You bloody fools . . .' he hissed. 'How many times have you been told . . .' He let go of my arm, and walked slowly along the hut, disappearing from view around the corner. I just stood there, half wishing he would come back so I could tell him that we had never meant any harm, that we had only been fooling about, but I knew he wouldn't come back. It was too late for words.

On the eve of Kres's funeral I was approached by one of my fellow trainees. He may not have been sensitive to people's feelings, but he was certainly shrewd in his timing.

He had a favour to ask of me, he said. There was no way that he would be able to cope with the theoretical papers which we had to sit. He might just be able to struggle through some of the easier papers, but there was no chance of him passing the three hour navigational plotting exercise. Would I help by taking the paper and then signing his name on it? But what about me? Well, I could resit the examination two days later under my real name. Then we would both have received our wings. I was too shattered to give the matter any thought, and agreed to his suggestion.

The exam came, and we swopped the navigation paper. Predictably, I was told to take mine again. Three days later the results were listed. For what satisfaction I could extract I found that I was still in the first five names on overall marks out of sixty students, and above average on Oxfords.

Kres was buried with full military honours. I carried the coffin along with five others. It was not very heavy. They had found some buttons, and a clamp from his jacket. As we laid the coffin down in the silent chapel, something clattered inside it.

...eral of an air gunner killed
...crash at Henswell
...nber Command). Geniek
the foreground.

...lackpool, soon after
...ining wings; Polish eagle
...orn by J.F.J's friend.

...Oxford in flight.

Blackburn Botha.

Avro Anson.

CHAPTER FOUR

Staff Pilot

Until the recent turn of events I had begun to feel bored by the endless thronging of train-loads of people into Blackpool and by the sight of the crowds milling non-stop along the streets and promenades. Frustrated by the long wait for the completion of pilot training, I often saw myself coming to Blackpool fully trained, proudly displaying my wings.

Now I arrived with less aplomb and panache. I had had a glimpse of the realities of wartime flying. I no longer felt like a seventeen-year-old boy, but at least the nineteen-year-old my documents said I was. It was near to the Autumn Bank Holiday, and I watched the crowds with a feeling of satisfaction. Unlike the southerners, whose reaction to the Poles changed with each passing fashion, here at least the northerners still thought Blackpool to be a magical place, and accepted the Poles as part of the fixtures, perhaps like the curiosity stalls on the promenades.

I found billets with Rysiek and a few friends of his, some of whom had qualified in the Polish SFTS. In between the flying assignments we had as good a time as I can remember. One parade per day, and Fire Watching Duty once a week were all the RAF expected from us at the time. The other Poles tended to patronise me in a rather fatherly fashion, which had its advantages. I made many friends, and passed the time talking endlessly of flying over morning coffee.

In the afternoons and evenings we worked our way through the shows and cinemas. We would often top this up by taking in Feldman's Show, opposite the Central Railway Station. For sixpence we would sit on the front row, watching the tableaux of

49

nude girls posing tastefully in yet another unique Feldman creation. The girls were skinny, and looked cold. There was always an excess of volunteers offering to remedy the poor girls' plight.

The finale had even us gasping . . . The very same girls, now dressed as nuns, sang 'Ave Maria' sweetly, eyes modestly cast down. This inevitably brought the house down, the ladies in the audience weeping unashamedly.

The young people in Blackpool were of course as hasty and impatient as ever. Most couples did not believe in long engagements . . . One day as we trooped into the dining room of our billets, ready for our tea, we were hardly surprised to see a young couple, in the back yard beneath the windows, in the process of making passionate love, regardless of the surroundings.

However, the Poles could not forget the war for long, nor its effect on our families. The war which was presented to us by the British news was one which we could hardly recognise. We had our daily ration of brave young fighter pilots receiving yet another 'gong' for conspicuous bravery. Apart from the fighters one of the other 'safe' topics was the war in the Middle East. Perhaps having failed to match the Germans in Europe, the battlefields of the Middle East could be viewed with a little more equanimity. The fighting tales of the desert had been romanticised by T.E. Lawrence during the First World War, but we could see no romance there, nor any charisma in Rommel, and we did not whistle 'Lili Marlene'.

The news from Europe always seemed lacking, to say the least. The only activities which people heard about seemed to be those of the Maquis. Europe ended after France, or so it appeared.

Bomber Command was one topic where we were wholeheartedly with the British. We realised that there was an incalculable value to the RAF bombers flying nightly over Europe, particularly at a time when most people on the Continent felt that they were losing their fight for survival. To those in the occupied countries the enemy seemed invincible, his resources unending, and his arrogance beyond challenge. For many in Europe the only tangible contribution from the West appeared to be the bombing missions and Churchill's stature as a defiant leader.

What hurt us most was that the real and greatest horrors of the war continued to be ignored by the West, which somehow seemed incapable of coming to grips with the extreme suffering of people living under German occupation.

Our interlude did not last long enough for us to become bored with it. Some three weeks on, at a morning parade, postings were read out for six of us, including Rysiek, Wartan and Myszko. We were not going to Bomber Command, as we had expected, but on to the staff of the newly formed Air Gunnery Training School. I do not think that any of us were disappointed by the posting. I had just less than 150 hours of flying to my name, and did not feel that I yet had the confidence to handle a bomber on an operational flight with six crew on board.

We had a celebration binge at the Winter Gardens, on the upstairs balcony. Among the many attending was a fellow trainee who distinguished himself not so much by getting monumentally drunk, which all of us did, but by throwing up, the results of which finished up on the unfortunate orchestra below us.

Perhaps it was not entirely his fault; the crowds between us and the cloakrooms were extremely dense. In any case, it seemed more appropriate that one should be sick over strangers rather than one's own friends, or so we consoled ourselves when asked to leave by the disgruntled manager.

Soon we were away to our new postings

*

Initially, at least, Morpeth proved to be somewhat of a disappointment. A hastily built aerodrome, it was located some twenty miles from Newcastle, close to the Northumberland hills. In the fashion of the day the contents of the station were scattered freely around the countryside. Our living quarters were nearly a mile from the messes, which in turn were another mile from the aerodrome. The runways were laid out at the base of the hills – perhaps to say laid out is slightly incorrect – the runways were cut through woods, and built on a bog. There was one hangar, and a curiously off-centre Flying Control, which, considering all the obstructions, was not very effective. This station was about to become the new Air Gunnery Training School, flying Blackburn Bothas and Westland Lysanders. The latter hardly need an introduction, but one has to be something of an expert on World War Two aircraft to find even a reference to Bothas. The fact is, they were basically an aberration, properly rejected by all the services as unsuitable for operational flying, then thrust upon a number of air training schools, particularly Air Gunnery.

The Bothas were all metal, high wing torpedo bombers, taking a crew of five in each plane. It seemed to us that a scrap metal dealer or a ship designer had been involved in their construction. The whole aircraft could be made absolutely watertight, submarine fashion. The torpedo bay was off-centre, the wings small, and the engine so underpowered that any pilot who flew one will no doubt remember it to this day. Two hapless Bristol Perseus XA engines struggled with the monumental weight, and with its awkward aerodynamic profile the maneouvrability was of low order, while the landing speed matched that of the most sophisticated aircraft.

However, we were young and keen to fly anything. We could not even be put off by the incredible noises of the hydraulic system. . .

Our standard crew was three pupil air gunners and an instructor, the pupils taking it in turn to fire from the upper turret at a drogue pulled by a Lysander. The firing ranges were over the sea, not too far from Newcastle. The town itself was taboo for flying, it being an important harbour, something we did not have to be told too often. The air above the town was packed with barrage balloons, and we had observed the anti-aircraft guns in action on occasion, not necessarily against hostile aircraft.

I went solo on the Bothas after two hours, having to relearn the whole landing circuit. The height was 1,500 feet, and the landing approach required a great deal of engine power, the latter always being used liberally to prevent the aircraft from falling out of the sky. This had been ingrained into me by our instructor, a tough local lad, now a flight sergeant, with a wife and small child. I followed his instructions and various asides to the letter, for I had an inkling that he had worked out a survival drill for this particular plane – survival being the operative word.

On Sunday, 24th October 1941, at 0700 hours, the first three aircraft took off in the morning mist. From then on, day in, day out, three aircraft would take off on the hour, the last landings being carried out in the evening shadows. The very first flights were for air to sea firing only; one flew at 100 feet above sea level, parallel to a line of floats. The instructor watched and corrected the pupils in their first firing of guns from the air. For the pilots it was an hour of crossing, turning, levelling out and recrossing the range, the noise and the smell of the fired guns mixed with that of the sick pupils. The trip, repeated three times per day, tended to be enough for even the keenest among us.

Before the sun set the first day we watched the first accident, a forced landing directly after take-off, by Rysko. We saw the aircraft wobble, heard the engines splutter, and in seconds the plane had disappeared behind the hills. The ambulance and the crash party tore away noisily, returning with Rysko. He was unruffled, and in time for his second trip of the day.

The next day we commenced what was to be the mainstay of our flying – air to air firing. This needed continuous alertness on the parts of both pilots so as not to become tangled in the long drogue wire, nor to get too close to the Lysander and give the pupils a chance to shoot it down. As we often flew in bad weather, the 400 yards long line constituted a serious problem. There was little room for mistakes. Within four weeks of the start little Myszko turned the wrong way at the wrong time. One of the Botha's propellers became entangled in the drogue line. The aircraft turned over, and dived into the sea. The Lysander crashed on the coast and burned. The body of Myszko, minus every single possession from his pockets and his person, was returned to us for burial. There had been no survivors in either of the aircraft.

*

On Tuesday, 11th February 1942 all the Poles on the station were told to report to the Flight Office. Once there we were faced with a small, middle-aged flight lieutenant, who wore thick glasses and spoke in a somewhat squeaky voice.

'Gentlemen,' he said, 'I am your new Polish Senior Officer. My name is Wnucki.' We stood dumbfounded. The Polish HQ had come up with another coup it seemed. This was obviously a way to reduce its top-heavy staff. The silence was broken by Wnucki, who circulated, shaking hands. He wore the ribbon of only one decoration, the Virtuti Militari. Later, when we snooped out his flying book we discovered that he was certainly no armchair pilot. Since 1940 he had been flying as a ferry pilot, had flown three times as many hours as any of us on some twenty different types of aircraft.

We also learned in time that in a chance medical both his short-sightedness and his small stature were questioned. He was shuffled out of the Ferry Command, but by pulling strings he had managed to get himself posted here to a job which allowed him to carry on flying.

He subsequently made no attempt to introduce any special rules. He regularly invited us in pairs to dinner, which was prepared by his wife. For the eighteen to twenty-year-olds the mysteries of a relationship between those in their late thirties were not to be fathomed. Their evident fondness for one another was therefore not even a topic of discussion for us. If we did draw any lines of separation from Wnucki and his wife it was on our not joining in their nostalgic recollections of the prewar days.

Two other Poles joined the staff soon after Wnucki. One of them was something of a dilemma for us for entirely different reasons. He had been a regular NCO in the army; he was not a very good pilot – in fact he disliked flying. Until then such people had not been found among us. He had volunteered to fly for the rank, the pay and the privileges which the wings undoubtedly carried.

Coincidental with his arrival, we in the mess began to gamble, playing mainly poker. I joined in of course, and within weeks lost not only all the money I had and would have in the foreseeable future, but also all my saleable goods including my bike. From then on, unless I managed to get a lift, I plodded a minimum of six miles a day regardless of the weather conditions.

In due course he came to what many of us considered his comeuppance. One day, while on my daily trek to the aerodrome, I heard a sudden crash followed by the bells of the ambulances and crash parties. A crash had indeed occurred: he and Wartan had taken off from two different runways simultaneously, could not see each other nor be seen by Flying Control. They met, and hammered into one another in the middle of the aerodrome. As a result of the encounter all that remained was a twisted head of metal. Yet somehow, out of eight aircrew involved, only one was seriously injured.

The crash was his fault entirely. Apart from the preflight briefing, there were various large signs indicating to the pilots which runway was in use, plus a duty pilot with an Aldis lamp was always present at the start of the runway. He was suspended from flying, pending an enquiry, then was grounded and posted to another Polish unit. He never lost his aircrew classification, and so he stayed working as a duty pilot for the duration. Thus he had achieved precisely what he wanted, although not exactly along the path he had originally chosen.

Apart from such minor interruptions we carried on with our flying as normal. We now felt sufficiently confident to enjoy our daily flights, coming back with all six aircraft in formation, joining in the bedlam over the aerodrome, where six other aircraft were in the process of taking off and formating. As there were no radios at the time, the confusion which ensued in such situations was often hilarious. On other occasions we would be caught out by sea mist, which made it essential to return at low level, pounding over the main streets of Morpeth, up into the hills, and finally landing with full drill from some 100 feet. Despite the frequent mix-ups and hazards, I recall no accidents from that period.

*

Neither the preoccupations with our own day to day problems nor the excitement of flying could completely reduce the impact of the relentless flow of war news, particularly as most of the RAF stations had better than average access to a whole range of information sources.

Our background obviously influenced our responses quite heavily. We avidly followed the rapid rise to strength of Bomber Command. The first one thousand bomber raid over Cologne was a measure of consolation for the news from Poland. In March 1942, twenty-four of my contemporaries were hanged publicly in the Town Square of my home town. Three miles from my home, in a cement works, a subsidiary camp of Auschwitz was established. Among the officials was an SS officer renowned for his inventive variations for disposing of recalcitrant or slow camp inmates.

Such news, as well as the reports of defeats and retreats in the Far East, made it hard to note the significance of the decisive victory for the American Navy against the Japanese at Midway.

Equally of little immediate effect was a letter from Geniek regarding the fate of a Polish Squadron stationed at RAF Hemswell. The squadron in question was the 304. Having suffered heavy casualties, the squadron had been selected for transfer to Coastal Command. The transfer took place on 14th May 1942, the squadron joining the 15th Coastal Command Group, stationed at RAF Tiree.

I knew but vaguely where Tiree was. Momentarily, I sympathised with the people I knew in the squadron, now posted to some inaccessible place on a distant island.

For us at Morpeth it was still possible to enjoy social life. We travelled to Morpeth regularly, attended weekly dances, and came to know many local people. But an invitation to tea by the local WVS, which was to be presided over by the vicar, threw us off balance. One evening we asked Wnucki to the Mess.

'I do not see what your problem is,' he said. 'Surely you have all been invited to English tea before?'

'Yes, but . . .' someone started.

'Well?' said Wnucki, rather sharply – he tended to be sparing with patience where stupidity was concerned.

'Well, the vicar is ... a non-Catholic,' blurted Bronek at last.

That remark reduced even Wnucki to momentary silence. Here in Britain religious matters were fraught with delicate issues. Those of us who had trained with the RAF had on occasion been called upon to fall out of church parades. Together with the Jews and the Nonconformists we then stood at ease, with our backs to the C of E majority. They in turn prayed for a quick victory over the intolerant Germans.

'You're not invited there for conversion to the Church of England,' said Wnucki, finally. 'Merely to be sociable.'

Bronek and the others said no more. After all, Wnucki outranked us considerably. We all went, out of a sense of duty if nothing else. In the event, if anyone cut an odd figure, it was Wnucki himself. His diminutive size, thick-lensed glasses and heavy accent, far worse than ours, turned him almost into a caricature of the mannered foreigner. Despite our good intentions, we were relieved when the tea finished and we could return to the Mess.

At some stage, we established contact with some Polish pilots serving in various capacities on aerodromes in the Newcastle area. We were particularly flattered by visits from a Polish fighter pilot from 303 Squadron, attending a conversion course to Typhoons not too far from Morpeth. The roar of his fighter on take-off, and the fantastically steep angle of ascent silenced even the most talkative of us. Not quite the same as a take-off in a Botha or a Lysander.

Had we had any idea of what was to come, our visits to Newcastle would have been even more interesting. Particularly memorable was a visit to a submarine manned by Polish sailors, which intrigued us with its claustrophobic restrictions of space and the proliferation of valves, stopcocks and pipes. Having been generously treated with vodka while standing in a miniscule wardroom, I made a comment about the dangers of life on board a submarine. A brief silence followed while the sailors looked at one another.

57

'You must forgive us if we find it hard to believe that an Air Force pilot should make such a comment,' one of the sailors answered. 'Confined in a cramped space, thousands of feet above the ground, with a few metal rods holding your aircraft together, your safety margin is tiny. A single nut or bolt loose and you will hurtle to the earth in seconds. Absolutely nothing could persuade us to fly in such contraptions.'

We stood and stared at each other, both groups unable to grasp how otherwise normal people would volunteer to perform such irresponsible, if not suicidal tasks

*

At that point we had been on staff duties for six months. By the normal regulations of staff flying, people were posted after about six months, having made their contribution in exchange for acquiring experience. But somehow a hiccup had developed in the system, and no postings were forthcoming. In the long run we were to pay a horrific price for this oversight.

As time passed, the evening card games began to pall. We started to drink rather heavily, and with an increasing amount of noise. In the air we were over-reaching ourselves also, which would inevitably lead to trouble.

One day, on our routine flight, a particularly sharp pupil noticed we were being chased.

'Fighter. Three o'clock, attacking.' I threw the aircraft into a steep turn just in time to see a Spitfire diving at me.

For the next fifteen minutes we fought a fierce battle, climbing, diving and side-slipping. It turned out that the Spitfire came from a refresher course some twenty miles away, and the pilot was itching to practise his new technique on bombers. We had a marvellous time; we, the pilots, that is. Rather hard-facedly we watched the white-faced students stagger out of the aircraft on landing. To give them credit, they never complained After all, perhaps the foreigners were as crazy as rumour had it, so what could be gained by complaint?

Meanwhile, our evening drinking sessions were becoming so

popular that some of the wilder spirits from the officers' mess began to come up regularly for the singing and dancing, which went on late into the night. As our wild behaviour escalated, it came to be my turn to face the consequences. We had a new squadron leader in charge of training – a non-aircrew and a strict disciplinarian. It seems that I chose the day of his visit to the drogue dropping zone to indulge in a spot of low level mix-up with the departing Lysander.

The story had it that the Squadron Leader was flat on the ground on my arrival over the zone, and that the airstream of my departing plane threw pounds of mud all over his best blues . . . I cannot say whether this is true or not. The charge as read out to me was deadly enough; '. . . well below fifty feet . . . dangerous flying . . . eye witnesses . . .'

I started under close arrest, but Wnucki intervened. I was suspended from flying pending a court martial. A barrister, currently a squadron leader in the RAF, offered to defend me. The day before the court martial, he had me take my shortest haircut ever – I looked like an undernourished sixteen-year-old. By the time we had gone through my statement of the hardships I had experienced, and my escape from Poland across Europe, the court no longer had the atmosphere of a disciplinary action. Found 'not guilty', I was discharged immediately.

The two others were not so fortunate. One corporal who had struck a sergeant was reduced to ranks, and received sixty days' detention. The next case was even worse: a sergeant instructor, an air gunner who had just returned from an operational tour, had been accused of offensive behaviour towards a superior officer and was reduced to ranks. A few swear words at closing time in a pub did not seem to deserve such harsh treatment, and I felt desperately sorry for him. We met later in the pub.

'You lucky bastard,' he said, trying hard to hide his emotions.

Within the next couple of days came an announcement that the Poles were at last opening an Officer Cadet Training Unit (OCTU). A course there would take six months, and although my educational qualifications would have been good enough to get me in, I did not apply. Most of the others did, and wondered why I did not. Of course, with my assumed name it would have been foolish to draw attention to myself now that things were going so well on other fronts. If I did apply my documents would be checked in detail, and the discrepancies would be noticed quickly.

I was more concerned with what I considered to be a drop in my flying standards. I was spent up, and my impatience and carelessness brought more trouble down on me, though not of such a serious nature. Having misjudged my landing speed, I persisted in trying to land, overshot, but was lucky to have the mud on my side. It slowed the aircraft down after it had overrun the landing strip, and the only damage sustained was to the rear wheel.

It was the only damage done to an aircraft through my own bad flying in my flying career, but one way or another it put the writing on the wall. Within days a posting came through, to night fighters OTU. I was immensely pleased. We had a huge party, then Wnucki and his wife came to see me off at the railway station.

*

I spent four glorious days at No 54 OTU, RAF Chartershall lovingly examining the Beauforts, Beaufighters and Mosquitos. This was the real thing. And then another Pole arrived. His name was K. Jaworski and he had trained with me at South Cerney. Fearing for the worst I rushed over to the HQ.

I was correct. Sorry, a mistake. Somewhere in the Air Ministry, someone has mixed up the initials. There was no doubt where E. Jaworski had been posted to; RAF School of General Reconnaissance, Squire's Gate, Blackpool. I should have been there nearly a week ago, so step on it . . .

I could not imagine feeling any more depressed, but I had to go, and before long I stood at the Guard Room of the Squire's Gate aerodrome staring in disbelief at the slow, graceless yellow Ansons of the Training Command. I was here to train as a navigator. Apparently Coastal Command, to which I was to make my way, now required the captain of the crew to qualify also as navigator. But not just any navigator – they had to possess a full Second Class Navigator's licence.

Back to the training then. This time around we lived in requisitioned luxury hotels. The course members came from as mixed backgrounds as I have ever seen; Norwegian naval pilots training for flying boats, Czech navigators for the long range Liberators, Dutch pilots, Free French and two Poles to fly on unspecified missions, and of course RAF to fly Sunderlands, Photo Reconnaissance Mosquitos or Spitfires. In numbers, the navigators predominated, and there were only two NCOs.

I was not impressed. I was still moping over the Beaufighters and the Mosquitos from which I had been deprived merely because of one initial. With bad grace I began to work, and instantly realised that this was no ordinary course. Having missed a week of flying, lectures and various other assignments, I would now have to work very hard in order to catch up with the others.

The course was intensive, starting at 7 a.m. and lasting until 9 p.m. each and every day of the week. Night flying came on top of those hours, and there was no time off during the day. To most members, the course was a step forward in their careers, and they were particularly anxious to maintain the pace. For me this was another 'self-motivating' exercise . . . the irony of finding myself from the position of staff pilot to confused pupil did not escape me. I felt miserable and self-pitying as I staggered towards the prehistoric Ansons, gasping with the weight of the parachute pack and the navigator's clobber, watched critically by a dandy pilot in leather gloves, a supercilious look on his face. Or perhaps it was just cynicism? To make matters worse, as our Anson had no hydraulic system, one of us had to wind up the undercarriage by hand, 149 turns after each take-off.

At first I could not catch up with pace in the air. We would drone on above the Irish Sea, inevitably towards Chicken Rock on the Isle of Man. Also inevitably, the pilot would treat us as morons. I certainly felt he was right, but lacking in equanimity I was not as happy as one. I worked frantically, calculating and plotting corrections to the courses prepared on the ground, taking drifts, recalculating ETAs, recording everything in the log book, and passing the corrections to the pilot. But on the way back the pilot would make for Squire's Gate so fast that we would have great difficulty in winding down the undercarriage before the plane touched down.

I was more confident of myself in the classes. There we spent many hours sitting in tiny cubicles which surrounded the 'sea', on which tiny toy ships moved slowly across guided by WAAFs. The merchant navy was escorted by equally tiny warships. Battles were fought, ships and U-boats sunk, aircraft shot down, and even smaller dinghies appeared. Our job was to identify the ships, estimate their speed, direction etcetera, report the data in coded messages then follow the received orders. Here proficiency in rapid identification of both Merchant and Royal Navy ships as well as German vessels, together with that of relevant bombers and fighters of both countries was essential.

About a week after my arrival I received a telegram; a close friend from Morpeth had been killed. I could not attend the funeral and waited for an explanatory letter. Instead, another telegram arrived: 'Rysiek killed. Funeral Tuesday. Letter following. Signed, Wartan.'

I read and re-read the telegram. This just could not be right. Rysiek – level-headed, intelligent, cool enough to land a Botha safely after engine failure on take-off. No, there had to be some kind of mistake. Wartan's letter was heart-rending. Rysiek, it seemed, was coming in to land, and was already over the runway, less than fifty feet from the ground when the Botha nose-dived but recovered. The engines roared up and the aircraft climbed steeply, hesitated, and with engines on full power crashed into the runway killing Rysiek and two pupils. The cause was apparently badly frayed control wires, which fractured at that moment. What made the story worse was that Rysiek's father, an RSM in the Polish Army, had been in India until recently. Having located his son, he obtained a posting to Britain. He arrived in time for his son's funeral.

Rysiek's death moved me deeply. I had been hard hit when Kres was killed, but in a different way. I had been a part of their personalities, just as they had been a part of mine, although different facets of ourselves had inter-acted with one another. It was perhaps just as well that the busy routine of the school kept me from too many self-pitying indulgences.

The assortment of people on the course offered as good a spectacle of odd characters thrown together by the exigencies of war as one could wish to find anywhere. The ever-correct Norwegians looked even more perfect in their faultless Navy uniforms, and then there were the 'Continentals', who in contrast wore what had originally been RAF uniforms, but which now had undergone numerous strange modifications.

The most eccentric among the latter was a Czechoslovakian flight lieutenant, who was invariably late for the morning lectures; the reason, as I had it explained to me by another Czech, was that he had a wife and children living with him – but they were not his own, and this caused some manner of unspecified morning complication. Anyway, upon his arrival each morning he would sit down at the back of the lecture room, open his brief-case, take out the daily paper, spread it carefully on the floor and carry out a meticulous inspection of his feet, clipping his toenails in the process. The English, perfectly capable of coping with such moments, carried on as usual, the lecturers never faltering. It should be said that I flew with the flight lieutenant, and his high level navigational proficiency made my work appear to be that of a half-wit.

Although never completely at ease with my role as navigator, by the time the course neared its end my ETAs coincided reasonably well with the Actual Time of Arrival (ATA). Night navigational flying, which turned out to be a considerable test of nerves, was mercifully infrequent. One of my flights took place in rather bad weather. For the entire flight I had no visual contact with either the ground or the stars. Only the wireless operator (w/op) saved me from difficulties by supplying me with numerous

Radio Direction Finding (RDF) bearings at regular intervals. The pilot flew on instruments for the whole flight, and to our relief we emerged out of the clouds close to the Blackpool Tower.

More memorable was an exercise carried out in thick fog, which was always particularly dense around industrial areas. We were returning from the direction of Anglesey at a respectable height of 5,000 feet, seeing nothing below us when a puff of smoke suddenly appeared level with the front of the aircraft. Two more, closer now. I could hear peculiar noises above the sound of the aircraft.

'AA flak,' said the pilot. 'Fire the colour of the day.'

'Balloon barrage,' I said, struggling with the Very pistol. We were in trouble. The AA continued blasting at us extremely accurately, the fabric on the port wing disintegrating. The engines howled on full power as the pilot tried to dodge the balloons, which were all around us now. We climbed westwards as fast as the engines would allow, firing the identification signals as we went on. Pure luck saw us through without any crew being injured, but the aircraft was badly in need of repair.

The course was to finish with a day of written and oral examinations. I studied hard, but like a few others I was gripped by another spell of gambling. The night before the exams, the worst of the gambling fraternity decided on one final half-hour game, just to relieve tension. Absolutely no longer, they said. An international team of six players sat down to the game at about eight p.m. At midnight we decided we would definitely finish at two a.m. We broke up at six a.m. I came out dazed, dazzled by the sunlight, but having won a small fortune. Mercifully, I passed the exam, and duly received my Navigator's Licence.

As I was packing my bags a telegram came for me: 'Wnucki killed. Funeral Thursday. Wartan.' I made straight for Morpeth.

The funeral was a splendid affair. As a holder of the Virtuti Militari and a friend of many high ranking officials, Wnucki's funeral brought people from all over the country. Officers arrived from London, the Polish Navy sent a detachment of sailors from a ship in Newcastle. Wartan and I were among the coffin-bearers. But it was not easy to look at the heavily veiled

(right) A group of Polish
aircrew outside their billet.
? is on the left.

(centre right) Polish aircrew
outside the Blackpool billets,
1943.

(bottom right) A group of u/t
aircrew 15 SFTS (P), RAF
Carlton. W. Moszoro is on the
right.

(below) J.F.J. at the funeral of
a Bomber Command aircrew.

Wellington Ics of 311 (Czech) Squadron.

Wellington Mk X: pilot's cockpit with dual instruction controls. Many additional instruments were added to the panels in the Mk XIV.

widow. At the end of the ceremony, when my turn came to approach her, she kissed me on the cheek, and holding my hand, wished me luck and God speed.

Later on, Wartan told me what had happened. Wnucki was returning from an air to air exercise when a Pilot Officer took off and struck the Major's aircraft from below. A wing was cut off, and both Bothas plunged to the ground, killing all ten occupants.

I travelled from Morpeth to Hemswell. Geniek had finally attended another medical, and had been passed fit for flying duties. There had been considerable head-shaking over his medical records, which did not seem to fit in with his physique at all. Now he was about to be posted to Blackpool to the No 11 IFTS.

It had been a long time, and we were both glad to see each other. Geniek was very cheerful, and far from envious of my wings.

'You've made a right balls-up of it,' he mocked. 'We were supposed to be fighter pilots. Now look at you. Anyway, I'm certainly going to be one.' I cringed, feeling slightly guilty, for I knew that Geniek was not happy about my tendency to follow the wild men of flying.

At Hemswell I watched the black Wellingtons of Bomber Command with mixed feelings. 1942 was not an easy year for Bomber Command; flying in obsolete aircraft, which the Wellingtons were by then, facing extreme navigational difficulties and a well-developed German anti-aircraft defence, the losses of Bomber Command were heavy. For the Poles, with four bomber and ten fighter squadrons the losses at that time created particular problems; the Polish forces in the West were out of manpower reserves, especially where highly trained or skilled personnel were required.

Not until 1943, when 100,000 or so of the Polish troops released from Russia began to join the Polish Forces in the West could the authorities bring in the replacements for the lost aircrew. But that was yet to come. At the time things were different.

Even during my visit, near the end of my leave, a Polish bomber in which Geniek's friend was returning from an operational flight, crashed while approaching the runway, killing the whole crew. Geniek and I escorted the friend's fiancée back to her home following the funeral.

CHAPTER FIVE

First Steps in the Squadron

In August 1942 came my first operational posting. For an aircrew this was a momentous occasion. Whatever had happened until now in his flying career was of little consequence. There were of course ways to delay the posting, but as far as most Poles were concerned only those obviously above the age limit were likely to avoid operational flying. The mounting casualty list meant that the Poles had to bring in all available aircrew to the operational squadron.

My posting was to the 304 (Polish) Squadron, only recently transferred from Bomber Command to the 19th Coastal Command Group in Dale, South Wales. The choice of one of the four bomber squadrons for Coastal Command was almost certainly related to the difficulties the Poles were experiencing in replacing their lost aircrew.

The squadron, together with others, was required as the Battle of the Atlantic moved towards the critical stages. Shipping losses could not be maintained at the level they had reached at that point in the war. Various anti-U-boat measures were being developed, and an increase in aircraft patrols formed an essential part of the plan.

Naturally, I was unaware of the various factors which led me, together with another pilot, Sergeant Wito, to make my way to the squadron. I knew that I did not want to fly heavy aircraft in general, and particularly in Coastal Command. Yet in due course I became greatly involved with the flying of the squadron, and with the experiences of those around me. As we lived so closely together and were isolated from the non-operational staff, there was hardly anything which we did not learn about one another. We felt keenly the shared experiences, both the enjoyable ones and the tragedies.

We arrived on a grey, cloudy morning, and were deposited along with our kit bags outside the sergeants' mess. This was a long wooden hut, painted various shades of brown, about a mile distant from the aerodrome. The countryside around was barren moorland. Close to the aerodrome large, black aircraft squatted in the circular concrete dispersal points. We watched one of the aircraft, slow and ungraceful, lowing like a cow, coming in towards the runway. Having seen enough, Wito and I entered the mess.

Wito was about the same height as myself, but thinner, so that his battledress hung on him scarecrow fashion. He had a mop of badly combed fair hair, and his green eyes seemed to take in everything at a glance yet remain focussed on some distant sight. One could see that he held an attraction for women, and judging from his unblushing confessions he had accepted offers of help from various quarters . . . At the time of our arrival we had in common the dislike of having to join the Coastal Command, and of being posted to a place like this.

The air in the mess was heavy with cigarette smoke, and there was the odour of men and unemptied ashtrays. Groups of airmen sat around tables playing cards and talking loudly. Nobody paid any attention to us.

I was dismayed, but hardly surprised. I could see at a glance that the Poles here were considerably older than ourselves. They would be pre-war regulars, and as such would not be inclined to enthuse over us when we arrived here wearing the badges of the RAF. It was obvious that we were the first of the Polish pilots to have been trained completely in Britain.

*

At the time of our arrival the squadron was not equipped for the specialised anti-submarine duties of Coastal Command. In fact, an attempt was being made to convert the squadron into a torpedo-carrying one. A number of crews were sent to be trained in torpedo strike techniques. The others continued to fly the anti-submarine patrols in Wellington Mk Is. The planes were still in their Bomber Command camouflage paint.

The aircrew seemed rather bewildered by the change. At that time and for some time to come I was in fact better trained for the operations than anyone there. However, with a typical wartime series of events I was not even allocated to a crew. Considering that among the many changes taking place was one in which each crew was being increased to six by the addition of a second pilot, I am not certain how this oversight occurred. Meanwhile, crews with single pilots flew operations of eight to ten hours' duration.

With so much reorganisation taking place, we found few people with any interest in us. We had of course reported to the correct officers, and attended all the parades, but no clear need for us had emerged. Meanwhile, more of the experienced crews left for torpedo training. The torpedo training posed a real problem. Everyone knew of the losses which the Beaufort squadrons suffered – one unlucky operation and they could be all but obliterated. What advantage could there be in using an aircraft which was even bigger and slower for the same purpose?

While these problems were manifesting themselves the operational flights continued at maximum effort, and some very dramatic air action was taking place. The intensity of the war on and above the sea in the Battle of the Atlantic was reaching its peak.

The flying mainly involved deep sweeps into the Atlantic or patrols over the Bay of Biscay. The aircraft of the time were equipped with depth charges, but were without any special aids for the detection of U-boats or help in the safe return to base of the aircraft, coming in at low level after ten or more hours over the Atlantic, often in bad weather.

The squadron which I had joined was known as the Silesian Squadron, which coincidentally was the part of Poland which I came from. Ironically, Silesia is the part of Poland most distant from the sea, and includes the Carpathian mountain range, which is some four hundred miles from the Baltic Sea coast.

The patrols from Dale were primarily directed towards the Bay of Biscay, where the action was rapidly intensifying. The idea was to attempt to hamper the U-boats in their courses to and from their French harbour bases. This action proved so effective that the Germans began a series of counter-actions, one of which was to send a considerable number of primarily long range fighters, such as the Junkers Ju88 and the Me110 to the Bay area. Thus the Luftwaffe fighters were patrolling the whole air space from north of Norway to the Spanish and Portuguese coasts.

At the same time the Germans speeded up their efforts to equip the U-boats with aircraft detection devices, and to install additional anti-aircraft armaments on the decks of the U-boats.

In August 1942 the squadron attacked U-boats twice, the second attack receiving a formal confirmation from the Admiralty, a feat far more rare than the actual attack. However, by September the attacks on our aircraft by the German fighters escalated, and our losses began to mount. We all had additional training in aircraft identification, lectures on fighter combat, and more air to air gunnery practice for the gunners. The old Wellingtons, flying at 1,000 feet, had no easy task fighting and throwing off the German planes.

While listening to the experiences of other people, Wito rather deviously worked on various members of the crews. The result was that one evening, early in September, Wito pulled me over to the Daily Routine Orders, grinning all over his face. His name was listed as that of a second pilot for his first operation. At first I was furious, then just envious – and anxious. Somehow I could not see myself fitting in with the old men of the squadron. The aircraft looked absolute beasts, and the struggle to become a captain impossibly slow and complex.

At 4 a.m. next morning the duty airman came to wake Wito up. I knew he was nervous, so I pretended to be asleep. He dropped things, and shifted about noisily. When he was ready, he turned towards me.

'See you in the evening,' he said. I heard the aircrew van outside, then silence fell again.

The day passed without anything unusual happening until lunchtime.

'Well,' said one of the sergeants, a gunner I had spoken to before, 'it looks like your friend's flown into trouble.'

'What's that?'

'They've sent an OA at 12.15. Two Ju88's.'

'Where were they?'

'Just about the middle of the Bay.'

I said nothing. What was there to say? I had no real conception of what was involved, even though my imagination worked overtime. God, what a trap. And no funeral with full military honours at the end of that kind of encounter. Not ever. The day collapsed for me. I smoked non-stop, and when I heard the familiar engines at 14.00, I could not think whom it could be.

I could hardly believe my eyes as I watched the old cow coming in slowly, touching down on the grass, then collapsing in a cloud of dust and smoke next to the runway. The ambulances moved in, and people were taken away. It must have been at least 6 p.m. before Wito, looking pale, made his entry into the mess. The air gunners came in at the same time, and were surrounded by their friends. Wito did not know anyone but me really, and he looked hurt at the lack of interest in his story.

He was not that articulate when he told me about it, however. It was not until much later that I realised that this being his first operation he would be confused and disorientated, never mind the Ju88's.

'I couldn't see anything until they practically sat on our heads. They gave us such a wallop. The intercom was full of jabbering – three o'clock high, six o'clock low. Then it went dead, just the roar of the engines, tracers, clouds, the navigator all bloody, me being sick . . .'

I preferred not to ask questions.

The next day, after the squadron parade, a little man

approached me. He was pasty-faced, fragile looking, his eyes watchful. But then, most Poles in those days were cultivating emotional abscesses.

'May I introduce myself?' he said, bowing politely, shaking hands with me. 'Could you spare me a minute, please?'

I listened, astounded. He was a first pilot, a senior one at that although only a flight sergeant. His second pilot was going to the OCTU.

'Would you like to fly with us as a second pilot?'

'But of course,' I answered immediately. 'I'd be honoured.'

He nudged me and smiled. His teeth were stained yellow.

'A diplomat, eh? As well as a qualified navigator and former staff pilot. Splendid.'

I was not so sure. I was certainly confused. We went to meet the rest of the crew. I was now with the establishment, it seemed. The navigator was a major, and like the rest of the crew, a prewar regular. There was a deep gash across his cheek-bone, the result of an aircraft crash in the distant past. The wireless operator and the two gunners were much younger, but even then a gap of about five years existed between us. We smiled and shook hands, as the formalities required.

However, it was some time before we flew together on an operation. The pilot had a story, although I never heard it from him in full. He had been a pilot in Bomber Command, and had flown eleven operations before being shot down over France. He found a way back through Spain, but had told no one the details. He said he was not certain what had happened to the rest of the crew; even if they had survived as POW's, they were unlikely to communicate with their former pilot.

Wacek volunteered for more operational flying, but was allowed only into Coastal Command. I discovered that Wacek was not all that well. He needed regular medical treatment, hence the slowness in getting on the operational flights. During the waiting I fumed, playing endless bridge, and becoming very proficient in snooker.

The squadron crews continued transferring to Docking for the torpedo training. I managed to sneak in a few test flights with various crews. Compared with the thorough way in which the Bothas were made, the Wellingtons were very sparsely finished. The fabric-covered structure looked fragile, inside all the connecting pipes and electrical wiring were bare and unprotected. The long wings flapped in flight, and together with the fuselage, would distort under stress. The aircraft were of the old Bomber Command type, with two machine guns in the front and rear turrets, and dual controls. The Mk X had two additional Brownings in the fuselage, one on each side.

Wito, meanwhile, was posted again for his second operation. As aircrew was entitled to go on leave every six weeks, and receive supplementary pay for the period after an operation, Wito was talking of taking leave soon.

At the time I began to realise how competitive the crews were. They shrewdly analysed each other's flying in detail, not necessarily very kindly. In Coastal Command flying, the crews saw two members as being very important: the navigator and the pilot, in that order. Any errors on the part of the navigator could easily kill the crew by bringing the aircrew down on the French coast or in the Channel, or towards the Irish Sea, to end up ditching or spattered against a mountainside. But in trouble, it was the pilot who was expected to get everybody out of difficulties with his 'sixth sense'.

From what I could gather, Wito's crew had no outstanding individuals. They all seemed nice-natured, ordinary folk. There was some head-shaking over the performance of the navigator, but nothing definite. The lesson of Wito's first flight had been a hard one, and he was excited but also more wary. The sky over the ocean was not as empty as it might seem.

This time I did not pretend I was asleep, and helped him collect his gear. After all, by then I had a crew of my own, and they seemed even more peculiar.

It was evening before Wito's aircraft landed. They had been up for over twelve hours. Apparently, after a long foray into the Atlantic, they came back well off course, and made a land-fall over an unrecognised coast. Finally they broke the radio silence, and asked for a fix. They were on the south-west Irish coast, close to Fastnet, and from then on it had been a long struggle back, using up the petrol reserves.

The German fighter activity over the Bay continued unabated. A crew disappeared without trace. Our attacks on the U-boats increased. Then one of our crews was attacked by two Ju88's some 250 miles south-west of the Scilly Islands on a clear day at 1,500 feet. The crew fought off the fighters, and returned in their shot-up aircraft with a badly wounded wireless operator. Next came a more sensational encounter: while close to the Spanish coast a crew was attacked by six Ju88's. Spectacular flying, excellent gunnery (one enemy aircraft shot down, one damaged), and a stroke of luck in the form of cloud cover saved the crew. It took three hours to bring the aircraft, its undercarriage knocked out, to Predannack, where the pilot crash-landed.

Wacek's name appeared on the DRO's, only to be removed after two hours. Then came Wito's third flight. By then we knew one another very well. We would spend hours sitting outside our hut, while Wito played the same record – 'I Cried For You, Now It's Your Turn To Cry For Me' – over and over again. Wito laughed at my outbursts of fury, but would not explain why he played it so often.

The day was clear, the sun shone. I sat outside the hut reading until lunch-time. When I entered the mess, I bumped into Wacek.

'I'm afraid your friend is in for it this time,' he said. 'They broke the radio silence, and asked for a fix. They were four miles south-west of Brest.'

I had my lunch, then sat behind the card players. Someone from the Intelligence looked at me:

'They've transmitted an OA message,' he told me. Someone bought me a pint of beer.

'The German radio from Brest has just announced the shooting down of a British Bomber. Two 109's got it . . .'

We waited. Tea time came, ETA, Overdue, Missing.

Missing. I took a mouthful of food, left the rest, and finished the meal with a cup of tea and a cigarette. I looked around. People sat in groups, talking animatedly, gesticulating. All the non-flying NCO's sat together. I stared at them for a long time. There they were, stolidly munching the tasteless food, not showing any signs of emotion at what had just happened. I felt resentful. I knew they felt smug, reminded of the short-lived glamour and glory of the aircrew.

When I looked at the aircrew, I could tell that they were discussing the fate of the missing crew. Some wore smiles on their faces. At the time I might have mistaken the meaning of these smiles, but I came to realise that they were the reactions of people who knew death, but once again were looking at it from the right side.

In time I was to learn to separate personal grief and emotions from the professional aspects of the extinction of a crew. We would speculate at length on the possible causes of each crew's disappearance or crash. Each crew was completely on its own, from its first operational flight to its ultimate end, however it occurred. We needed to try to unravel at least some of the mystery of such occasions. The reality of finding ourselves in a similar situation was too close to be ignored.

There was no question of sending search planes out so close to Brest in the daytime. In the evening two crews took off in a search, but returned with no information.

The next day when I came back from parade, Wito's bedding and all his belongings were gone. The only person to be notified was his girlfriend, if she still remembered him.

*

Almost immediately we were listed for an operational flight. I eyed Wacek anxiously. He looked pasty-faced, but perhaps no more than usual. I hoped that we would go at last. We did.

I slept badly that night, and smoked heavily the following day. There was an atmosphere of unreality over the whole day. I followed the progress of the crew, watching for clues. The gunners wore their Irvine jackets and trousers, Wacek packed a pistol in his flying boot, the rear gunner a long sheath knife. I saw no sign of excitement nor of the feeling of unreality in the others. To them it was all very real.

In the briefing room there were only three crews. Rarely would there be more, and except for one short period only one crew would be taking off at any given time.

The crews examined their routes into the Bay of Biscay with great concentration. All routes went to the Scilly Isles, then diverged in approximate south-westerly directions. Ours was marked A-258, and as befitted the most senior crew was the closest to France. Locations of U-boat sightings and attacks were shown, but at least as much interest was focussed on the reports of fighter activity. We were to fly within the range of all the types of German aircraft currently active over the Bay —long range Ju88's, Me110's and even Me109 single engine fighters. Beaufighter patrols were due in the morning and in the after-noon. Aircraft of ours missing and shot down in the previous twenty-four hours included a Whitley and a Wellington, both close to the Spanish coast.

I ate the operational breakfast of two rashers of bacon and a fried egg with relish, astonished to see the navigator give his por-tion to the rear gunner. 'Old man,' I thought to myself, but I was not to know that giving up such luxuries had nothing to do with age.

The ground crew were courteous. 'Let me help you, Mister Sergeant,' they would say, carrying my heavy pack into the air-craft. We shook hands, and they wished me luck. Wacek meanwhile spent some time adjusting the pilot's seat and the controls to fit in with his diminutive figure. By then the sun was rising. The day promised to be cloudless, the wind sock was hanging limp. We were ready. I sat down on an auxiliary seat next to the pilot. Wacek spent the minimum of time checking the engines, and taxied immediately away. His flair for knowing whether or not the engines were sound was unparalleled. The green light for take-off was waiting for us.

Wacek lined up the aircraft, pushed the throttles forward steadily and fully. He held the plane on the brakes for what seemed like ages, the engines roaring and the aircraft shaking. At long last he released the brakes, and the aircraft began slowly, ponderously, endlessly to ascend. We barely came off the runway at its very end, at once over the coastal rocks with the sea beneath us.

'Course 255°,' said the Major. I set compass while Wacek did the post take-off drill. We hardly climbed any higher. The aircraft seemed to wallow in the still air. By then the sun had risen. We were on our way.

An hour later we were heading towards the Bay of Biscay, having set the course from the Scilly Isles. The weather was still perfect, the sea smooth as a mirror, the sun growing hotter rapidly. The crew was completely silent. The usual drills finished, the guns tested, the Identification – Friend or Foe (IFF) signal switched off, there was no chatter of any kind. Both gunners kept the turrets turning slowly around, the major navigator stood in the astrodome searching the sea and sky. Even Wacek was silent.

'Fighters attacking a Sunderland,' said the wireless operator.

'Where?'

He gave the position. Nobody commented.

Another hour passed. We smoked and had coffee. Then Wacek called me, and after a bit of a struggle I was at the controls. Initially I had considerable difficulty gaining control over the aircraft, since it turned out to be extraordinarily heavy on controls. To keep the plane on the course required continuous checking and rechecking of the gyro against the magnetic compass.

We were flying at 1,500 feet and I seemed to have hardly settled in when I heard the intercom.

'Aircraft, two o'clock, low, five miles.' This was not going to be my day. I looked anxiously at Wacek, who was adjusting his binoculars in the given direction. Without looking at me, he put his hand on my shoulder. I sat still, nervously checking the course.

'Descend to 1,000 feet,' Wacek told me.

I became immersed in the technicalities of readjusting the height, but Wacek gestured impatiently, and I pushed the aircraft into a shallow dive.

'800,' he said.

'I simply cannot take fighters on,' I thought.
'500.'
Not a cloud in the sky.
'Beaufighters,' said the rear gunner.
Reprieved.
'Stay at 500,' Wacek said. I was not happy, but did as I was told. The sea was close now. I looked up when Wacek touched me, just in time to see the Beaus in a steep turn around us to starboard. Lucky swine.

I stayed at 500 feet for a long time. Wacek disappeared into the back of the aircraft, came back, sat down and dozed off. At last he beckoned me to climb back to 1,500 feet. Then we changed over, and started changing courses, finishing up on a north-easterly one. Now back across the Bay again. The sun was high, the cockpit hot. I was wilting. And still you could cut the tension with a knife.

'Fighter attack,' said the wireless operator. We listened to him relaying the message without comment.

I could see no point in it. 'Damn morbid,' I thought. Stuck in the middle of the Bay of Biscay on a cloudless day, broiling in the sun, and so far in five hours all we had done was change courses, and hear who was getting shot down and where. With an imagination like mine there was too much time to think in this kind of flying. I lit an umpteenth cigarette, poured another cup of coffee for Wacek and finished mine. I began to think what an odd organisation the Polish squadrons in the UK really were. Letting my mind wander I missed the impact of another 'shot down' message. This time the aircraft had been attacked only a few miles from us, and had belonged to our squadron. The whole crew had got the chop.

The front gunner saw the Scilly Isles from some incredible distance. We had by then descended to 200 feet. The patrol was nearly finished. The crew continued their silent vigil right to the moment Wacek made one of his smooth and flawless landings. That was it. I definitely disliked this kind of flying. Neither my age nor my temperament, my flying abilities nor previous flying experience fitted me into this squadron.

I do not recall making much fuss over it. The crew was polite to me, if still slightly distant. Not so Wacek, who treated me as if I were the squadron mascot. After all, we had come back, the others had not. He chatted up the WAAFs and two eggs appeared on my plate. He treated me to his cigarettes. Naturally, I enjoyed the attention, and only understood later what a complex person Wacek was. From me he wanted not the flying ability which he knew he had himself, but another contribution which he knew that we all needed in order to survive and prosper – luck.

Perhaps reflecting the rapid changes which Coastal Command was undergoing at that time, the squadron was again in doubt concerning its future role. Although the bulk of the squadron had gone to the torpedo conversion unit at Docking, rumours already had it that the authorities were going to change their minds again. But whatever the rest of the squadron was going to do there was no torpedo training for us. As the first step to the proceedings, we were sent on leave. Having done my first operational flight, I was now entitled to more frequent leave. At the first opportunity I was off to see Geniek, who was stationed at the Polish IFTS in Blackpool.

I was back amongst the Blackpool Poles, who loved to spend hours in cafés or restaurants, sipping a coffee or a beer, talking interminably, eyeing up the girls, fancying what their chances might be.

CHAPTER SIX

Over the Bay

Thus came the year 1943. The war had by then engulfed the world. The hardships and experiences of wartime living were seemingly shared by all nations, but was there really anything in common between Americans at home complaining about the difficulty of buying nylon stockings, and the state of Russian POW's in German hands? And how does one judge the restriction of movements imposed on the Swedes or the Swiss compared to those of a Pole or a Jew in a concentration camp?

I travelled to Blackpool on leave with Wacek and Jan, our air gunner. Next to me, Jan was the youngest member of our crew. We got on well, but were rarely on the same wavelength on matters such as interests and outlooks.

Wacek, in his best blue, showed all his decorations for the first time. He had a Polish Cross of Valour with bar, and British Military Medal, the latter, I surmised, related to his escape from the continent. Wacek's luggage on the journey was reduced to a minimum, mainly because he nursed a basket of eggs all the way. These had been painstakingly collected from the local farmers over the past few weeks, and now we formed a guard around him as we jostled our way north. They were a present for his fiancée in Blackpool, about whom we knew nothing other than the fact that she lived in Lytham. The last I saw of him he had boarded a taxi, still cradling the basket in his hands.

I made for Geniek's billet, where he had booked a room for me. I found him much cheered up now that he was on the way to his flying career. We had a long talk about my present flying predicament, but Geniek could think of no escape from the clutches

of Coastal Command for me. We both knew that the worst thing
for either of us would be to draw the attention of the authorities.
All I could hope for would be to try to change to twin-engined
fighters, without creating too much fuss about it. The best course,
it was decided, would be to finish the tour then apply to an
Advanced Flying Unit (AFU) for twin-engined fighters. We drank
to that.

By the time of my visit, the inevitable reaction against the Poles
had reached the north. Geniek suggested that I should spend a
few days in London, where the presence of so many Allied troops
reduced the pressure on any one nationality and its individuals.

Of course, we had begun to view the English with more than a
few misgivings by then. Isolated on their little island, crowded in
their tiny houses, working in the vast industrial towns saturated
by heavy industries and full of smoke and grime, the English
were totally different from any other nationality we had met.
Unsurprisingly the problems of Europe were well outside their
interests, their response subject mainly to what the media said at
any given moment.

Our interest in the war and its progression continued to be
much more than intellectual. The growing power of Bomber
Command was to us a great morale booster. The ignominity of
the Dieppe raid we could barely make ourselves read about.
Such a foolish and bloody venture flew in the face of the realities
of the war. And the bad news seemed to continue, until I began
to envy the English who could turn to the sports page of the
newspapers first.

The news of the Warsaw Ghetto uprising came, and of its sup-
pression. The horrors were all the more poignant to us because
time after time we had heard about Polish anti-Semitism. The
truth is that the Jews were subject to as much antagonism in
Britain as anywhere else in the world before the war. The reasons
for it were numerous, including the relentless propaganda of
prewar Nazi Germany, which spilled over the whole of Europe.
The border area where I come from had as its inhabitants not
only Poles but Germans, Czechs and Jews. It would have been
inconceivable that any national group could become involved in

activities against another.

The extermination of the Jews on Polish territory had brought a double nightmare onto the inhabitants; a mandatory death sentence for anyone aiding the Jews was but part of the pressure applied. The life and death decisions that the average person had to make in his day to day living were not the armchair dilemmas which so often occur in the West. We were all fully aware of the scale of the exterminations taking place in Poland, and the ghetto uprising piled the anguish on further. How long would it take for others to start to listen?

After the usual stop at Pauline's RAF station I made my way to London. On the way I heard about the Ruhr dams raid. This was the RAF and the British at their best, but I felt that my nose was being rubbed in the mess again. In a somewhat chastened mood, I started on my way to the squadron, only to discover that my destination was now its new location, RAF Davidstow Moor.

It was a long journey, and when I arrived I had nothing to cheer about. Located on the Cornish moorlands, with not a tree in sight, the aerodrome was brand new and very functional. Built at the bottom of an incline, one of the two runways faced a steep hill. At the end of the other runway was a bog. As with Morpeth, the station was dispersed over a large area of country, and appeared to be just as hastily built. The Wellingtons still had the Bomber Command black camouflage, and torpedoes filled a number of dispersal points. I rushed into the mess to find out what we were up to now.

Nobody seemed certain of what was happening. The whole squadron was now back together at the base. What type of operational flying we would be taking up remained to be seen. During my absence on leave we had lost two crews, one on an operational flight, one in a flying accident.

Within a couple of days we found out about our new tasks: white-painted Wellingtons began to arrive, carrying a row of aerials on top of the fuselage, and 'whiskers' close to the front turret. These were the Wellington Mk XIII, equipped with ASV Mk II (see appendix). This was the first step in re-equipping and training the squadron for the specific task of anti-submarine warfare.

It was a relief when the conversion from the black Bomber Command Mk X Wellingtons to the pristine white Mk XIIIs began.

Obviously, there were times when I was not due for an operational flight, and with Wacek's bouts of illness, these seemed to become more and more frequent. During these periods I spent my time like any other aircrew; I would stay in the sergeants' mess until late, playing bridge or snooker, or just chatting over a beer. It was often after midnight before I would start the walk along the narrow, muddy path to the distant sleeping quarters, as the corrugated iron huts were somewhat grandiosely called.

One such night, having fallen asleep in the cold, damp air of the unheated hut after undressing in the darkness, I was suddenly aware of being shaken.

'Wake up, Mr Pilot,' said an unknown voice. It was quiet but insistent, as was the shaking of my arm. A torch was shining in my eyes. I groaned and tried to turn away.

'Wake up, wake up.'

I struggled to full consciousness. 'What on earth is happening?'

'You're on an operation. You're flying.'

'What? When? Now? What time is it?'

'It's 2.20 a.m. Hurry up. Your crew's already being briefed.'

'What's going on?

'No idea. Come on, you'll have to be quick.'

He shone the torch while I scrambled frantically around, trying to gather my clothes and dress without waking anyone up. I struggled into my battledress and flying boots, but had no time to put on any warm underwear. I paused for a minute, then took my sheepskin jacket.

I stumbled out into the cold night, still not really sure that I was awake. I lit a cigarette and followed the Duty NCO to a small van. He drove silently but speedily to the Briefing Room.

The Briefing Room was full of noise and bustling people.

'Ah, here he is,' I heard the Major say. 'Good afternoon, Mr Pilot.'

The crew stood in a group, fully dressed in their flying gear. They looked at me blankly. Wacek came over, a solicitous expression on his face. That look generally meant that a dangerous operation was in the offing, or that Wacek wanted a favour performing for him. He looked paler than usual, and had large, dark rings around his eyes.

'It's all set. Everything's okay. The briefing is over. We've got all your gear. We didn't have time to send for you earlier. It's all rush, rush, rush. Let's go.'

He gave me a sickly smile. I must still have been staring in amazement, because he added:

'I'll explain later. Here's your food ration. Unfortunately there is no time for a meal.'

I followed him out. There were two more crews waiting for the aircrew van. Once in the van, nobody spoke. At the dispersal point we unloaded near a black Mk X. It looked sinister in the darkness. The ground crew was still loading bombs on, not depth charges, I noticed.

Wacek was already in his seat. He quickly swept through the cockpit drill, started the engines and was taxiing off before I had secured the parachutes and the rest of the gear. I could not stand the suspense any longer.

'What's up?'

'A blockade runner. Coming in from Japan, making for Bordeaux. Carrying rubber.'

I tried to take the information in. That explained the bombs and the old Mk X. The other crews would be right at home with their Bomber Command experience. It did not appeal to me at all, but at least I had better knowledge of ship recognition than the others.

By the time we reached the take-off point, I was trying hard to imagine why the cargo was so important. Rubber? From Japan? All that way – what the hell was the point?

'Stand by. Take off,' said Wacek.

I had given up trying to cross-check his pre take-off cockpit drill. He gunned the engines until the aircraft vibrated and roared. He let go of the brakes, skilfully controlled the swing to starboard, and we were off, rolling. Then came the red lights, the end of the runway. The moorland hill was somewhere ahead.

I pulled the undercarriage up. Wacek was already starting a slow, climbing turn to port in order to avoid the hill. The clock read 2.45 a.m.

'Course 195°,' said the Major.

I set the course on the compass.

'On course,' said Wacek.

Evidently we were not going in formation, for we made no attempt to wait for the other crews. The orders seemed to be proceed individually, to identify and to attack the target. It was also clear that speed was essential, for we now flew at a speed twenty miles per hour above economical

Wacek stayed at the controls. We flew no higher than eight hundred feet, and once over the English coast began to descend into the darkness. Our course would take us very near to the French coast.

I found it very difficult to pull myself together. Disorientated by the suddenness of the events and the scant information, I tried to piece things together and to visualise the sequence of the forthcoming events. Firstly, I had to give up on the cargo of rubber; it seemed incongruous and lacking in seriousness of purpose. It soon dawned on me that the Germans would be hardly likely to sit by while the RAF came in and bombed a valuable ship. By 3 a.m., with no food in me, I had a clear vision of the ship, and the blue sky above it buzzed with Me109s and Focke Wulf 190s. I shivered.

It was a cold night. Wacek would not have the heat on. Worse, he had opened the side window. Without any warm underclothes or gloves, I was not exactly comfortable. Had I been in Wacek's position on this flight, I might have felt somewhat warmer. I lit another cigarette.

'Stay alert,' Wacek shouted into my ear. 'We're nearly level with the French coast.'

As far as I could make out, we were practically on it. Flashes of anti-aircraft fire to port, searchlights on and off; the Germans were awake and alert.

Wacek dived still lower until I preferred not to look at the altimeter, particularly since so far out from base, we could not correct the setting for the changing barometric pressure.

Once the active part of the French coast was behind us, we turned still closer in until the dark mass of land was visible. Wacek flew low and fast, not sparing the petrol. There was little chatter in the aircraft.

'Here is the exact position of the ship,' said the wireless operator, suddenly.

'It's definitely making for Bordeaux,' said the Major. 'Our ETA is seventy-two minutes.'

The time was 5 a.m. Already a faint strip of pale light was appearing over France.

'Stand by for enemy aircraft,' said Wacek.

The gunners' turrets began to swing methodically from port to starboard and back again. I scanned the dark sea anxiously.

The French coast was becoming more clearly visible. The Major corrected our course to keep us further away. The aircraft seemed to be hopping from one wave crest to another. I glanced at Wacek's face. His concern was obvious, and echoed my sentiment – we were in for it this time.

At thirty minutes to the target, the Major passed me on the way to the bomb aimer's panel. I watched him expertly adjust the settings on the panel. He avoided my eyes on the way back.

It was full daylight now. I thought that we must have looked aggressive and purposeful – a black bomber speeding so low over the sea. Looking at Wacek, I began to speculate on how I would pull him out of his seat once he was hit. I had no doubt that he would be.

Twenty minutes to the target. I lit a cigarette for myself and one for Wacek. No more after this one.

Fifteen minutes.

Ten minutes. It must be just over the clear horizon. Any minute now and we would have have visual contact.

'Message from the group,' said the wireless operator. He

sounded breathless. 'The strike is cancelled. All aircraft to fly fifty miles, at 270°. Start anti-submarine sweep as of now. Then, course for Scilly Isles.'

'What? That can't be right,' said Wacek. He shook his fist at the horizon. 'This is unbelievable.'

Nobody said a word. I was not capable of another emotional response. The hours of building up towards the climax of a tricky attack were more than enough, particularly as I had been convinced that this one was our last.

I took over once we were on the new course. Wacek went for a conference with the Major and the wireless operator. The weather stayed clear all the way back to the Scilly Isles. We saw only one solitary Sunderland making tracks in a south-westerly direction. I had to admit to myself that one aircraft alone above the vastness of the sea looked terribly vulnerable, and far from threatening.

We landed back at base at 10.30 a.m. The mechanics grimaced at us, but said nothing. Wacek immediately rushed over to Operations to find out what had happened. I did not wait around.

I stumbled back to the hut, crawled into bed, and was asleep almost at once. When I woke up, I found it hard to believe that the flight had even taken place.

The next day, when I saw Wacek, I avoided the subject of the flight, and he never mentioned the outcome of his visit to Operations. I never did find out what became of the ship carrying rubber from Japan to Bordeaux.

*

Wacek took me on some dual trips, which gave me the insight into the flying characteristics of the new aircraft. He had just returned from a few days on a conversion course, and we were soon assigned to do an operation.

The flight proved to be an anticlimax. We followed a number of radar contacts, but to no avail, even though the flight was made in daylight. The radar operators argued over the manipulation of the radar, which then settled the dispute by packing up with a loud blast. Peace descended on the crew. Everyone was now back in their positions, scanning the air and the sea more anxiously than ever.

I sat at the controls for nearly nine hours of the flight. The more powerful engines and the additional aerials once again changed the flying characteristics of the aircraft. At the same time, highly controlled and accurate flying was now the order of the day. Otherwise, the new equipment would have been little use. This may seem obvious, but many of the older pilots found it hard to adapt to the increase in demand for very precise course, height and speed control over the whole length of a long operational flight. The lesson was taught the hard way, if no other, since the culmination of pilot and navigator errors could be dramatic.

Nearing England, we found clouds in profusion, which at first suited us until we discovered that the base was in cloud right down to ground level. On most occasions, Wacek preferred to take risks rather than break the radio silence. Now, having located the Scilly Islands with some difficulty, we circled them almost at sea level.

'Damn it,' said Wacek. 'Ask the Group for instructions.' The wireless operator took ages. At last there was crackling on the intercom.

'Diversion to Exeter,' he said. Wacek and I exchanged glances. That was fine for the Group, but how the hell were we going to find our way to Exeter with cloud at 100 feet below land level?

Wacek went to consult with the navigator. He came back looking unhappy. We changed over, and the Major gave us a course. Off we went into mist.

In the failing daylight we scanned the view ahead, straining to see a glimpse of land.

'Land ahead,' said the front gunner. We then started a series of course changes in order to stay close to the coast. Lizard flashed past to port, we corrected for Start Point.

'Lights flashing at two o'clock, on the sea . . . bastards are firing at us.' Wacek dived and pushed the throttles forwards, while the wireless operator seemed to fumble with the Very pistol for ages.

I was becoming impatient, but experience had taught me to keep my mouth shut. I caught a glimpse of a row of colourful sausages moving slowly out of the mist, accelerating towards us. At that moment, the wireless operator banged away with the identification colours, but Wacek continued with the evasive action. For a time he flew almost glued to the surface of the sea. We were past Plymouth, turning north towards Exmouth.

It was well for us that Wacek's low flying skill was so great. By the time we landed we were all rather shaken by the episode, but soon the crew were chatting about the radar as though nothing had happened.

It was part of the squadron's tradition that no badges of any kind were worn by the aircrew on their battledress, so that for an outsider it was impossible to tell who was of what rank, often with hilarious consequences. However, this was one of the occasions where our lack of badges produced slight chaos. The exasperation of the staff at Exeter was shared by us also. Next morning, the weather having cleared up, we made our way back to the bleakness of Davidstow Moor. Then, after some more dual training, we set off on another operational flight.

This time, our route went back to the Bay of Biscay, close to the French coast, making directly for the Spanish coast. During the various preflight stages I began to identify the crew's preoperation tension signals; Wacek oozed insincere jollity, kowtowing to the Major, and even buttering me up. The Major talked too fast, while the rest of the crew sat eating their operational breakfast in silence. For my part, I kept my emotions under control by smoking a lot, and saying far less than I wanted to.

In the Wellington Mk XIII, and subsequently the Mk XIV, there was no seat for the second pilot. One simply stood. Both our front and rear gunners went into their turrets before take-off, in spite of warnings. This, I surmised, was an inheritance from the bomber days, when German night fighters prowled over the

Bomber Command aerodromes. Being alive was preferable to obeying the rules of the air crew manual.

By then, the instructions for the use of the ASV (the early version, fitted to the Mk XIII) were that it was not to be used until the main patrol section of the flight. The simple reason was that it was tricky to operate, and could easily malfunction.

There was a great deal of cloud over the Bay that day. We flew through areas of stratus and some cumulus, varying the height from between 200 feet and 2,000 feet. Not far from Brest the rear gunner noticed aircraft at five o'clock. There was no response, but the crew was going through the drill, the Major alerting the wireless operator, and so on. I just stood and worried. In a flight I would be expected to pick up any crew function that might be required.

The silence seemed to last for ever. Wacek put the aircraft into a steep turn. The rear gunner started to say something. I had a quick sight of a trio of sinister-looking aircraft, moving fast against the background of white clouds. For my money, they were Ju88's. For the others, it mattered little. Just then we reached the clouds. We turned, once inside the cloud cover, and came out on a new course.

There was a long way to go, and this was not a propitious start to the patrol. Someone was bound to get caught out. It needed no complex thinking to work out the movements of an aircraft over the Bay. I opted for coffee and sandwiches. I did not want to consider the possibilities.

As time passed, the daily battle over the Bay gained pace, judging from the wireless operator's reports. There were sightings of and attacks on U-boats, air attacks, ditchings. The wireless operator, a serious, studious young man, did his duty as told; his was not an easy job. Cut off from communication with the crew over long periods, he had to put up with difficulties in listening to signals which came through badly due to low altitudes and long distances from Britain. We absolutely depended on him to receive the half-hourly Group messages, which often addressed individual aircraft, giving them new or different tasks, recalling them early or changing their destination. In addition, information

on attacks was of great importance to the pilot and navigator. All
the same, I disliked his constant stream of disasters, and thought
him overzealous in reporting them ceaselessly.

After a time we saw the clouds ahead signalling a change in the
weather. At first this was rather welcome. But with the sky
darkening and cloud level lowering, I saw our way blocked by a
solid mass of cumulo-nimbus criss-crossed by flashes of lightning. Wacek gave me one of his crooked grins. For whatever
reason, Wacek was not worried by bad weather.

We flew straight into it. And stayed in it. We had it drummed
into us that it was vital to carry on with the operation no matter
what the weather conditions were like, otherwise the enemy
would take advantage. Thus Wacek pressed on, believing that
our chances of catching a U-boat actually improved under such
conditions. That may have been so. The Group certainly
assumed that each crew would weigh up the risks and its ability to
cope with them by itself. For that reason the recalls by the Group,
although frequent, were related only to exceptionally difficult
landing conditions.

That day we flew through the violent disturbances into clearer
weather, but lower cloud ceiling. To our astonishment, the ASV
operator located the Spanish coast from twenty miles, with
visibility at 100 yards. At three miles from the coast we
turned back.

After about two hours, we came out of the bad weather. I preferred it, but not so Wacek. To him the enemy fighters constituted a greater threat than the problem of storms. We arrived
back at base after eight hours forty minutes – the exact time
allocated to our flight.

At the time of the squadron's conversion to Mk XIII Wellingtons,
U-boats changed their operational tactics. They attacked the
Allied convoys in 'wolf packs', staying together, often on the surface. They carried improved aircraft detection devices, and their
anti-aircraft armament was large and deadly. Confident of their
ability to fight off the patrolling RAF planes, they began to stay
more frequently on the surface and engaged the Coastal Command

aircraft in ferocious fire fights.

In order to deal with these tactics, Coastal Command experimented with a wide range of techniques and strategies. One of these was to send out aircraft in formations, instead of the customary single bomber. For a period this technique was used by our squadron. Being a senior crew it was inevitable that we would be one of the first to be assigned to the new patrols. We were to fly over the Bay on a daylight sweep with two other crews.

On the whole, the crews did not particularly welcome the formation flying approach. Having always flown singly, the crews had developed strong, individual attitudes to the operational missions. Of great importance was the 'survival and attack' routine which the crews would work out among themselves. The sudden switch to keeping visual contact with two other aircraft seemed to be the product of office theorising, and we had some difficulty in viewing the new tactics as realistic and practical.

Wacek was strongly against the idea, and spoke out strongly against it on many occasions. Now, as we stood in front of the DRO's reading the names of the three crews in our formation, his face was quite contorted.

'Look at those two crews,' he hissed. 'Neither of them has more than three operations to their name. I doubt if their navigators can find Land's End, never mind a U-boat.'

During the briefing we sat at the front to show our superiority, but as the briefing went on, we realised that the flight was going to be far from easy. Wacek looked even more glum as we listened to the complex procedure needed to ensure that we would stay together in flight, as well as attacking a U-boat without jostling one another out of the sky. We were to lead, but everyone was responsible for maintaining contact. I thought it would make a change from the usual anti U-boat patrols, and the flights were meant to last no longer than eight hours.

Soon Wacek foresaw every conceivable permutation of doom. He could barely hide his feelings whilst talking to Kaz and Jan, the two first pilots flying with us. However, Wacek shook hands, smiled, and generally paid an extraordinary amount of solicitous attention to the crews and pilots in particular, making some rather outlandish promises. Unfortunately for him, both Jan and Kaz took him at his word, and looked flattered by the attention of such a senior pilot.

'They'll never make it,' he said to us, almost triumphantly, a remark which quite mystified me.

We took off at 7.15 a.m., and climbed to 1,500 feet above the aerodrome to wait for the others. We had good weather; cloud base 3,000 feet, about 5/10 cover, visibility ten miles or more. Five minutes later we set the course for the Bay, with the other aircraft spread out in a very open vic formation.

My special task on this operation was to keep an eye on our friends, and report any signals sent by them. Already Wacek had intimated the impossibility of any rational communication with 'the likes of those two'. Accordingly he did not even glance at them, but pressed on as if we were alone.

For over an hour all was well. The weather stayed reasonably good, and to me at least the sight of two other aircraft was reassuring. Only too soon the complications began. The weather deteriorated to 10/10, low stratus. We descended lower and lower until we flew at between four hundred and five hundred feet. Sensibly, the other two aircraft closed in without any exchange of signals. For a time I rather enjoyed the situation. The three aircraft speeding away in formation would present an inspiring sight. I was certain that we would give the enemy a good run for their money.

Wacek and I were about to change places when the aircraft shivered. The engine noise changed. Suddenly the aircraft seemed to rear.

'Damn,' said Wacek. 'Engine trouble. Fire red flares. We must climb.'

This was less enjoyable. The port engine instrument readings went out of control, we lost speed. We flew into the clouds, tur bulent ones. We still held on to the original course. Wacek shook his head.

'Jettisoning the depth charges,' he said at last. 'Contact the Group. Message: Engine trouble, returning to base.' Then he added, to us, 'No smoking, jettisoning fuel.'

The decision to break the radio silence was difficult; besides being absolutely forbidden except in exceptional circumstances, there were also friendly aircraft in the vicinity. But soon we were on a reverse course back to England. The clouds were breaking up, and we flew into brilliant sunshine, with low, white stratus stretching below and ahead.

The starboard engine temperature was rising alarmingly, partly because Wacek was gunning the engines mercilessly. A very long two hours followed, the time seeming to stretch even further as we neared base. Then, typically, Wacek shut the engines high above the runway and descended in a stylish turn as we lowered the undercarriage on the way.

Debriefed, we settled into a game of bridge in the sergeants' mess during the afternoon. The Operations Room phoned: Jan had just attacked a U-boat!

Wacek dropped his cards, muttered something, and rushed out of the mess. He returned before dinner. We asked no questions, and he offered no explanation.

In the evening we were in on a game of snooker when Jan came in. His fresh complexion was flushed. He saw Wacek and came over to us.

'Mr Wacek, we were very worried about you.'

Wacek wore his crooked, vinegary smile.

'How kind of you, Mr Jan. But it was nothing, a triviality.'

'You know that we attacked a U-boat,' said Jan, earnestly.

'Well, well, do tell me.'

'She was diving. We just saw the conning tower disappear. We gave her a good hammering, anyway.'

'Hmm,' mumbled Wacek, nodding. 'Congratulations, Mr Jan. A fine effort.'

Jan bowed and left, no doubt to celebrate with his crew.

'A whale, I think,' Wacek said to us once Jan had gone.

Undoubtedly this was a touch of sour grapes. We all knew that an attack on a U-boat was a rare occasion, the icing on a cake. Within the next few days, the formation patrols ceased. We went back to individual aircraft anti-submarine sweeps. The Bay of

Biscay remained our operational area.

*

The next day we flew with Squadron Leader Korbut, our Flight CO, on a training flight. He was small, well built, energetic and incisive. He scrutinised our performance in some detail, then came to fly with us instead of the Major. Looking at the route on the morning of the flight, I concluded he was a real U-boat hunter. We were to practically hug the French coast all the way to Spain. Nobody seemed concerned, and I felt that I was worrying for everyone.

Korbut was full of energy. However, if he undertook a difficult task he did everything to minimise the risks involved. He certainly spent much less time at the navigator's table than the Major did. Most of the time he was either in the astrodome or next to the radar operator.

I had no sooner taken over the controls from Wacek when the radar operator said, 'Contact 240°, ten miles.' I glanced at Wacek. He nodded.

'On course,' I said. I began to lose height down to 500 feet. At six miles the visibility was good, but there was a strong wind. The sea was choppy, full of white caps which hampered the observations.

'A boat,' said Wacek. I dived to deck level, pleased that it was not a U-boat, and saw a fishing boat, its mast swaying. There was nobody on deck. We did not care much for this. We speculated that it was probably a German observation post. We photographed it, and went back to the patrol.

We continued flying in a south-easterly direction, closer to France again. The coast was just over the horizon, less than five minutes' flying time. For an Me109, that is.

At last the clouds came up on the horizon. This turned out to be the grandfather of storm clouds, and Wacek took the controls over. For the next eternal half-hour we bumped and heaved, the wings flapping wildly. No instrument needle stood still. I held on to the side window with both hands, while the floor under me

95

either disappeared or pushed up against me. Water poured through all the cracks in the cockpit until we were both thoroughly soaked. Then we suddenly came out, and I took over the controls. Once again, Korbut made us climb to the patrol height of 1,500 feet. The hot sun shone above us, the engines droned and the wireless operator chanted his litany of disasters.

We reached Spain, flew west for twenty miles, then turned on a parallel course northwards. I watched the clock, trying to work out the time of our passage past Brest harbour.

'Aircraft three o'clock, two miles,' said Korbut. Over Wacek's head I saw two minute aircraft silhouetted against the sky. I glanced at Wacek, but he gestured at me to stay at the controls.

'Permission to descend,' he said. I was already diving gently, levelling out at 200 feet, but Wacek pointed to the zero on the altimeter. I took the aircraft lower, until the sea spray began to cover the cockpit windows. The waves were moving fast, very close under us. The sea was huge, rolling restlessly.

I was sweating. Wacek followed the aircraft intently. 'Can Korbut get us out of this one?' I wondered.

'Hello, where is my bloody aerial?' the wireless operator wailed suddenly. I pulled the aircraft up to 200 feet, while Wacek's shoulders shook with a suppressed giggle.

We landed after just over eight hours' flying time. At mealtime the Squadron Leader stared at Wacek and me for a while.

'You damn clowns, you think you're clever,' he said at last. 'I'll take you two for a real ride down the Bay yet.' And he did.

We completed an uneventful operation two days later, and three days after that we were off again. Wacek did not feel well, and sat listlessly on the step next to me. I must have flown for nearly five hours without a break, and had just examined a ship some 350 miles from land when I realised that something was wrong. We were flying at 90° to our previous course, and the port engine was roaring. Engine failure.

Until now I had taken the engines working perfectly during an operation for granted. In fact, the ground crews in the Polish squadrons were first class. Their mainstay was the prewar regulars who had escaped from Poland, and now, after many years of experience were capable of overseeing highly reliable maintenance.

Wacek was now giving me instructions. Both of us were watching the speed. But the engine roared and milled. At 700 feet, with the speed falling, we changed over. Wacek jettisoned the bombs.

'Wireless operator: message to base. Returning, engine trouble.'

I watched Wacek struggling to stabilise the aircraft. Our speed was thirty knots below cruising. The starboard engine did not react too well to the extra power required from it. Its temperature rose. 800 feet. I looked at the sea. No place to land. The swell was enormous, it would be like hitting a concrete wall.

The aircraft was a beast to fly on one engine; the pull on the rudder required great strength to overcome. At this height all that could be done was to fly straight and level. Wacek hated feathering the propeller. It was so final. I hoped he would not have to, but the engine would not go.

After a prolonged struggle, we realised that we could not maintain the height.

'Feathering port,' said Wacek. I pressed the button, the propeller stopped. That was it, on one engine we did not have enough height to straighten the flight path for a ditching. I felt slightly sick, my throat went dry watching our peculiar crab-like flying position.

At last the wireless operator found the Scilly Isles on the radar. We had long abandoned the radio silence to let the Group home us in.

'Land ahead,' said the front gunner. We could land in Predannack. But Wacek would have none of that. We crept on at 350 feet, hammering the one engine all the way to Davidstow Moor. Landing, Wacek's speciality, was dramatic. We made straight for the runway in use until we seemed to be suspended high above its end; Wacek simultaneously closed the engine and pushed the undercarriage lever down. We dived, falling like a stone, the warning horn bellowing. I pumped like mad to accelerate the undercarriage down. At the very last moment the flaps came down, we ballooned, lost speed and touched down. This kind of flying was out of my class . . . And thus we returned from my sixth operational flight.

Bad news of a different kind awaited us on the ground. An incident in the German–Russian war was a portent of the troubled future for the Poles: the discovery of the mass graves of the massacred Polish officers at Katyn was a disaster of terrible magnitude, with far reaching consequences. Our emotions rose, and the political scene became even more sinister.

Locally, the gloom deepened following a crash. We had lost an aircraft recently when, following an encounter with German fighters, the pilot had landed on the boggy ground and suffered no casualties. The latest crash occurred during take-off. On a May morning we listened to the laboured roar of engines on full power in operational take-off. Then suddenly, silence. We rushed out in time to see the aircraft flop onto the hillside. There was no explosion, and we presumed all was well. Half an hour later we discovered that during a forced landing following engine failure the propellers had broken up, the crash killing both pilots instantly.

It was soon time for my leave, and I was off for a week. I was somewhat shaken, and less critical of the crew's competence. I was beginning to understand that each operational flight brought new elements into play, and each needed to be absorbed separately.

CHAPTER SEVEN

Last of the Easy Days

I spent the leave with Pauline. She was a good companion for such occasions, especially now that she had joined the WAAF. She was a sergeant, and obviously could have been promoted or commissioned, but was reluctant to do so at the moment. I did not press her for her reasons; there were grey areas that we did not touch on in our conversations.

When I arrived back, I found Wacek sick again. By then I had come to know some of the first pilots, and soon one of them approached me: would I go on an operation with them? They were the only all-NCO crew in the squadron at the time. The pilot, Kieltyka, was smallish, fine-boned, with a thin, ruddy-cheeked face and small bright eyes. He was always full of humour. The crew already had a reputation for their high standard of flying, for an attack on a U-boat and an engagement with German fighters in a brief but vicious flight. Following the last event, they had made their way back to Predannack, with a badly damaged plane and a wounded wireless operator, where they had crash-landed.

The flight with Kieltyka was set in a different phase of the war against the U-boats – the introduction of night patrols. With the coming of improved radar these were inevitable. The U-boats, under growing pressure during the daytime, used the night to emerge and recharge their batteries.

So off we went, for a night patrol close to the French coast, to return in the daytime. The crew was alert, very silent. There were no reports from the wireless operator, only the radar operator coming in. We checked endless blips and contacts, laboriously

99

working our way through the U-boat attack drill.

The next day I flew with another crew, chalk and cheese if ever the expression was appropriate. The captain's sloppy course-keeping was made up for by the excellent and unobtrusive navigation. I assumed that the navigator was well acquainted with the captain's foibles and managed to correct for them.

This turned out to be my last operation on the Mk XIII. Now came the real Coastal Command training on the Wellington Mk XIV. The aircraft was radically modified. In the middle of the fuselage a retractable turret was built in, containing a Leigh Light – a powerful searchlight – controlled from the front where a turret had been removed. The perspex nose now contained the searchlight controls, a fixed machine gun and under it, the latest radar's rotating scanner. In addition, the navigator was given a Gee box. Less happily, in the central bomb bay an auxiliary fuel tank was installed . . . We now had more powerful engines, which however only just made up for the modifications in the aircraft. But this aircraft was a far cry from the original Wimpy of the early days of Bomber Command.

The whole crew had to be retrained. The new radar was capable of locating a U-boat accurately at long distances, but needed a great deal of concentration. It was decided that no operator would sit at the radar for more than half an hour during an operational flight. Consequently three crew members became wireless operators–air gunners at hourly intervals.

The drill for night attacks on U-boats would be as follows: once a U-boat was seen on the radar screen, the second pilot went into the nose to operate the Leigh Light controls and the machine gun. The Leigh Light was turned on at half a mile from the submarine. At this distance the U-boat would have been lost on the radar due to the sea returns. The Leigh Light would have been lowered by the navigator when five miles from the enemy, while the pilot gradually reduced height down to fifty feet. At this height he would rely on the radio altimeter completely. From that time, the flying height for all operations, day or night, was 500 feet.

A massive training programme was required, and was started

at once. We spent many hours, day and night, training for the new aircraft. We soon found that, to go smoothly, the drill needed enormous amounts of effort. Nothing seemed to go right for a long time. The coordination of the whole crew required a new discipline. After six weeks of training our night exercises were pathetically inadequate. At one point the radar operators could not hold the blip long enough, losing it before the light could be turned on the practice sub. Or the searchlight operator, in this case me, could not hold the sub in focus because we were not lined up properly, and Wacek had to make hair-raising turns at the last moment. At fifty feet with the bomb door open and the turret lowered this seemed suicidal, at night worse. Another week of hard work, and we were ready to set off on our first all night operation. An uneventful flight of ten and a half hours' duration was recorded.

The next night we went out again. The take-off in these aircraft involved carrying a large overload, which meant that the total weight carried exceeded the limit allowed for landing. If an emergency occurred it would be necessary to drop the depth charges and jettison a lot of fuel before landing could be attempted. The operational take-off therefore became an important part of the whole procedure.

That night I took the controls after the take-off, and flew for five hours. I began to feel tired, and at 500 feet and some 400 miles from the coast one needed to be as alert as possible. But the intricacies of controlling the aircraft suddenly ceased to be of importance when, with a colossal noise, the starboard engine failed. Wacek was in my place instantly.

He needed to be. While the engine coughed and wheezed, spitting out showers of sparks and belching flames into the darkness, we were losing height rapidly. We lost more when we jettisoned the bombs. We sent an SOS. We were down to 340 feet, the estimated distance to England was 460 miles. The night was pitch-black, the engine refused to work.

This was indeed a harsh reality. When Wacek coaxed an extra 300 feet out of the aircraft we were seventeen seconds from sea level instead of ten. A further three hours of flying followed.

101

Several times Wacek tried to extract more power from the ailing engine, but it reacted furiously, and he gave up. We shook and vibrated our way to Predannack, coming in over the cliffs onto the fully lit aerodrome.

Once on the ground we talked only of the engine failure drill, and how to improve it in the future. No one could be allowed to feel sorry for himself in front of the rest of the crew. We all shared the same risks, and would share the same fate if anything were to go wrong.

The following day we returned to base. That night a crew did not return. 'Missing over the Bay of Biscay', later 'presumed killed.' Speculations over their fate would have been worse than unprofitable, but most crews made their own short-lists of possible causes.

Another day, and we were off to the Spanish coast and back, taking ten hours and thirty-five minutes over it. We were learning to use the radar more proficiently, and began to understand its contribution to the flight programme. When flying low all other navigational aids, including the Gee box, proved to be of but marginal use. The radar alone improved our general accuracy in the task of fighting U-boats.

I was rapidly adapting to the type of night flying the operations demanded of us. But the fatigue that descended over all of us in the early hours of the morning was difficult to overcome. By 3 a.m., with six or seven hours of flying behind us, it seemed impossible to fight off sleep. We smoked and drank coffee, but our eyes began to ache and the concentration was hard to maintain. By the first light of day we were all exhausted; we looked red-eyed, pale and drawn.

The next day after that flight we tested the aircraft particularly well. Korbut, now a wing commander, was coming with us. Then a Flight Lieutenant Zurek decided to fly in place of Wacek.

Wing Commander Korbut was a charismatic person, full of the qualities that serve leaders well at all times. There were no barriers in communicating with anyone on any topic. His direct approach was especially appreciated in an operational squadron where there was no room for humbug. Either one could fly operational flights, and fly them well, or one could not. The rest was irrelevant. Words changed nothing. The highest decorations were only for today. Envy was not evident until the losses began to decrease later in the war. Korbut's appeal was based on such sentiments.

That evening Korbut was at his best; he teased us, asked us questions, joked with us. He rushed us through the meal. In the briefing room I hardly dared to look at the route of E-198. I was not disappointed in my worries. We were not even flying to the Scilly Islands, the usual starting point of the patrols, but directly over Predannack towards the French coast. The rest of the crew did not seem too bothered.

We took off in the fading daylight. I was relieved, for I tended to distrust the ability of other pilots when flying at night with an overloaded Mk XIV if any trouble developed during the take-off. Soon we were struggling over the Cornish tors, seemingly only just missing them. As soon as we had heaved over the Predannack rocks I took over, descending immediately to 500 feet. The WingCo kept coming to look at us.

I chewed gum during that part of the flight. We could not smoke on the Mk XIV during the first one and a half hours of the operation because we were using the auxiliary petrol tank in the bomb bay. The aircraft was full of petrol fumes. The change over to the main tanks was somewhat unnerving. Most pilots waited until the engines had missed a beat, so to speak, before changing the tanks over. This time we were as close to Brest as I could ever wish for under the circumstances. We saw the searchlights over the harbour, and everyone was gaping at them when the engines stopped. I was at 250 feet when they began to work smoothly again, but already Korbut was on the intercom.

'Geniek . . .'

'Yes, sir,' I replied. 'I'm just going up.' I chewed at the gum furiously. 500 feet was too high for my liking, so close to the well defended French coast.

We changed over. I had coffee and a cigarette while watching our approach to a storm up ahead. At night such storms were most dramatic. Lightning illuminated huge towers of complex cloud formations, showing clearly the minute gap between the cloud base and the sea – our route. Zurek flew straight into it. Hail beat on the cockpit, water was seeping in and we were thrown madly about.

'Blip, eleven miles, 10° port.' I could not believe my ears. With the interference he must have had on the screen in this weather, how could anyone possibly see a blip?

'Good man.' said Korbut.

'On course,' Zurek said.

'Ten miles ahead.'

'Well?' Korbut said impatiently.

'U-boat, sir.'

'Sure?'

'Positive, sir.'

'Bloody big expert after six weeks on the radar,' I thought.

'Stand by in attack positions,' said Korbut.

The weather conditions were absolutely devilish. Zurek would not be able to control the aircraft below 300 feet even without the turret out and the bomb door open. Gusts of wind threw us all over, hail hammered at us. I made my way to the nose of the aircraft in time to see the white caps of the stormy sea by the light of the lightning flashes.

'Three miles, on course.'

'Turret lowered.'

'Geniek, I'll take over your position. You stand next to the Flight Lieutenant,' said Korbut. The engines roared up. Zurek needed all the power to keep the aircraft flying with the turret down. Korbut pushed past me, and I moved back in time to hear, 'One and a half miles ahead.' A ferocious bump. Zurek must be dripping with perspiration. I knew I was. 250 feet, a mile to go.

'It's gone, sir.'

'What?' bellowed the WingCo over the intercom at the poor radar operator. 'Gone? Gone where?'

'Just disappeared, sir.'

'Leigh Light on,' said the WingCo. A bright light suddenly illuminated our wing, then went out. The controls had not been adjusted, I thought anxiously. God, was that my fault? At that moment the beam came on again, illuminating the sea, white with the fury of the gale force winds. No trace of anything.

'180° turn,' the WingCo said. I watched Zurek struggle with the controls. The aircraft was rearing madly.

'On course.'

'Anything on the radar?'

'No contact, sir.' The WingCo swept past me. I knew he would soon be tearing at the poor radar operator. I felt sorry for whoever it was; to be shut in there in mid-fuselage, thrown around with the engine noise and vibrations being far worse than up front. Had he been sick on the radar, I wondered. However, not even the WingCo could conjure the blip out again, even after we had started a routine search as if it were an exercise off Lundy on a lovely summer night. But to no avail.

We went back on the patrol course. We changed over, and the weather eventually improved somewhat. After an hour Zurek took over again, and immediately flew into another storm. The rough weather now continued until we reached the Spanish coast, had a glimpse of the lights and turned back again.

We now flew against a strong westerly, which was pushing us towards France. The thunderstorms subsided, but the air remained rough, rain and hail coming back repeatedly.

When I took over again at two in the morning I was very tired. We had been flying, if that was the right word, for seven hours by then. The clock was hardly moving, we were half an hour behind our ETA and the fighter zone was still ahead. When Zurek took over he adjusted the engines to their most economical power level.

'Descend to 300 feet,' said Korbut. We were pushed for petrol, and had to fly very close to France, and the WingCo, standing by the radar operator and seeing how close to the coast we were, preferred to reduce our height slightly.

We did not stay down for long. Once the first daylight began to show over the eastern horizon the intercom crackled;

'500 feet,' said the WingCo. He had hardly finished speaking when the rear gunner said, 'Fighter', so calmly that at first I was not certain that he had said it at all. At once his four Browning .303 machine guns started up. The aircraft shook, the smell of cordite came wafting down to us. Zurek pushed the throttles forward.

'Don't,' said the WingCo. One could understand that. The sparks and flames were a dead give-away. Zurek was now in a steep turn towards the tracers coming at us out of the darkness. Our machine guns rattled away again. I could see nothing at that moment, but the continued fire-fight meant that the fighter was still holding on to us. We went in and out of the thin clouds, then into more continuous cloud cover.

'Aircraft, three miles, 75° starboard.' Still too close for comfort, but with the daylight on us we turned 300° northeast, towards England. Soon we were back to the economical cruising speed, landing at the base after eleven hours and twenty-five minutes of the flight.

After the debriefing the WingCo called me into his office. His eyes were red. He looked very tired. The gist of his talk was that I should have been sent to the OTU some weeks ago, but there had been such a need for second pilots during the conversion to Mk XIV that they could not spare the men. In two weeks' time there was another course starting at the OTU and I was to be on it.

However, before I left the squadron Wacek had recovered enough for us to take on another operation. It turned out to be a long and arduous trip. We took off and landed in daylight, but the rest of the ten and a half hour flight took place at night. We flew behind a front, so the skies were full of grey clouds and the white caps of the sea were lined up in a westerly. I struggled with the controls for nearly seven hours, checking out various radar contacts.

The visibility when approaching England on return was almost nil, but as long as the radar worked we no longer took the risks of the earlier days. No flying in at deck level, waiting for a glimpse of the coast then pulling up hard in order to avoid the rocks but not lose sight of the land. Now the radar operator guided us along the north Cornish coast until we were close to our base. Here we still had our fill of excitement, coming in at 100 feet over the familiar land-marks, sideslipping the heavy aircraft to Wacek's perfect landing.

In the operational canteen Wacek chatted up the WAAF. I was then presented with a huge multi-egg breakfast, my last as a second pilot.

*

A week on leave allowed me to visit some of the friends with whom I kept up correspondence. Geniek had by then started on his SFTS course at Grantham, flying Miles Masters, prior to the fighter OTU. His dreams were becoming reality. I did not visit him at that time because the initial stages of his course allowed no time off at all. He and I were due to complete our respective training at about the same time.

In London I met Wartan. He was a flying officer by then, and looked very elegant in his uniform, every inch a real airman. He had just been to the OTU as a second pilot and was on his way to a squadron. I noticed that he regarded my still being a sergeant as something of an indignity, but I was not quite clear to whom. I do not think that I felt any envy at his advancements. I had made my choice way back, and had allowed Geniek to take the brunt of the resulting frustrations. Now I had no regrets, except that I would have preferred to fly something like a Mosquito. But that was a relatively petty annoyance.

In Blackpool I met some other friends, now pilots in different squadrons stationed in most unlikely places around the country. We drank quite a lot, and engaged in flirtations with yet another batch of girls freshly out of the horrors of wartime industrial work and let loose for a week on Blackpool.

A new addition to the multitude of uniformed crowds were the Americans. We Poles got on with them easily and naturally. For a hundred years the USA had been the dreamland of Europe, the promised land – Utopia come to life. Millions in the USA had their origin in Poland, and periodically here some of the Americans spoke to us in Polish.

But Poles were aware of politics which transcended personal relationships, and to which their families and their country were unwilling hostages. The American Poles were innocent of the implications of the changes taking place in the world. They thought they had come to rescue Europe once again from calamities. They believed that, given their power and technological superiority, things would be all right in the end. The Poles from Poland were not so certain. The cycle of change was affecting everybody.

Remembering France in early 1940, we now perceived that the rights and wrongs of the European problems which seemed so clear to us were but dimly understood, the critical issues fudged and side-tracked. Not surprisingly then the traditional enthusiasm of the Poles for the Americans' way of political thinking was rather muted now. After all, there was no sign that anyone in the West spoke clearly for Poland.

Also, the dichotomy of being in England yet living elsewhere was particularly noticeable among the older generation of wartime 'exiles'. We preferred to keep to the here and now, especially with the bad news from Poland creating so much fear and anxiety. As time went by we thumbed our way through the seemingly endless stream of publications containing nothing but harrowing stories from Poland, and dissertations on the complex policies of a doomed nation. This was the language which no one spoke in the West, no one understood. We perceived the anguish of the older generation, but then our heads turned away. It seemed much better at times to look at and live in a 'real' world.

The English girls were lovely, no doubt about that. It did not matter that we could not engage in the more involved verbal bantering – it definitely did not affect us in the days of urgent living that war brings. The mating games of the Englishman seemed egocentric, that of a cockerel crowing in full plumage, looking for a grey hen. The Poles felt that they, in turn, tried to make the girl feel that she was the only one worth paying attention to, thus letting the girl decide whether or not she wanted to take their words seriously.

Thus, filled up with the somewhat unreal worlds of wartime London and the northerners' paradise – Blackpool – I departed for No 6 (C) OTU, located at Silloth. The OTU had a Polish Flight, of which Zurek had coincidentally just become CO. We liked each other quite a lot in spite of having flown together. At times I found his approach to flying too traditional. Not unnaturally he did not always enthuse about me: too forward and disrespectful, inclined to Anglicise unreasonably . . . Of great importance to me was finding the Officer Commanding Flying of the Polish unit to be Squadron Leader Ladro, a legendary figure who had, a few months earlier, fought four Ju88's in full daylight for an hour over the Bay of Biscay, in an obsolete Wellington Mk I.

Once again it was back to training. Here the aircraft looked to have been used hard and as if they had belonged to an earlier era of the war. One flight still flew Bomber Command Wellington Mk X, but Zurek told us that he was here to modernise and update the Flight. Mk XIII and XIV were expected to arrive in the not too distant future.

The flight's first parade was also an opportunity for all of us to see who the pilots, navigators, wireless operators and gunners were. Of the potential first pilots/captains of the crew there were two NCO's and two flight lieutenants. I almost certainly had the highest number of operational flights and most flying hours to my name; on the other hand I was not yet twenty years old, although I had flown in Britain for over two and a half years. While the crewing up discussions went on, I found that among the otherwise complete strangers there was a second pilot who not only came from my home town but had been my senior in the Scouts in the prewar days. We decided to fly together, although I felt that it was I who had been decided on to a great extent. Nikel was a down-to-earth, permanently cheerful person, round-faced and jolly. He fixed us up with a crew. In the afternoon we met: the navigator, a red-cheeked university student, was older than any of us; there was a wireless operator who seemed even younger than me, and two gunners trained also as wireless operators. We had the customary evening drink, then reported back the next day as a crew.

However, the rest of the crew was then assigned to a series of ground training programmes. It would be three or four weeks before the first pilot's training was suitably advanced to begin flying with the whole crew. That day I reported to Squadron Leader Ladro. I had already heard a great deal about Ladro before I met him, in particular concerning his battle with the German fighters. At that time I was quite obsessed with the idea of running into enemy fighters, which was hardly unusual considering that our squadron operated almost exclusively over the Bay of Biscay. There was always a high level of fighter activity over the Bay, and it was clear that our prime danger lay in the air and not in the sea. I lived in dread of becoming involved in a similar situation to that of Ladro's – it was impossible to envisage fighting a prolonged battle in the type of aircraft we were operating in. The stories of the old Wimpys returning to base in tatters were numerous, as were the numbers of aircraft missing, disappeared without trace, or known to have been shot down.

The aircraft was simply an open metal structure covered with fabric. Hardly anything inside was protected, and a single bullet in the right place was enough to destroy the plane. The feeling of being exposed and vulnerable was enormous, and if the pilot were to be hit at 100 feet, the chances of survival for the rest of the crew were negligible. With a wing span of eighty-six feet and flying at low level, the aircraft was very close to the sea indeed.

By the time I arrived at OTU there had already been several dramatic encounters with the enemy. On 16th September 1942, Flight Officer Stan Targowski from 304 Squadron fought against six Ju88 long range fighters in full daylight. The battle lasted for twenty-five minutes, and was a fine example of skill, nerve and tactics from the pilot and gunners. There were only two front and two rear turret Browning .303 machine guns to protect the Wellington Ic from close to twenty cannons and at least six machine guns in the German fighters. During the course of the encounter one Ju88 was shot down and another was badly damaged. The Wellington sustained considerable damage, but none of the crew was injured. But, as a tragic postscript, the entire crew with the exception of the navigator, who was off duty, perished at the hands of enemy fighters only a month later. The operation was the usual anti U-boat patrol over the Bay.

The aspect which troubled me most from the pilot's point of view was the necessity of physical strength and stamina for handling the aircraft. Long, non-stop, complex manoeuvring of a bomber was exhausting, and could not be sustained at length on later models of the Wellington. By the time I met Ladro the squadron was using the Mk XIV aircraft, whereas both Ladro and Targowski had been flying the Mk Ic, between which there was a major difference in handling characteristics.

In the hut to which Wito and I were allocated there was a flight sergeant air gunner named Wlad Piserski. He was a large-boned, seemingly clumsy man. He walked with a slight stoop, was quite withdrawn and slow to smile. Both Wito and I took to him, possibly due to the fact that his temperament was the antithesis to our over active and excitable behaviour.

One evening as we talked he was changing his shirt, and as he dressed we were silenced by his appearance. We watched in surprise as his back, chest and left arm were exposed, revealing long red scars of newly healed wounds. Our silence lasted only a short time. After some pressure Wlad told us that he had been the front gunner for Flight Lieutenant Ladro on the occasion of his battle against the Junkers. At the time Wlad was in the middle of his operational tour, previously having flown some fifteen missions with Bomber Command.

Once on the subject, Wlad had no reticence about discussing the battle. It had taken place on 9th February 1943, and his memory of the events seemed perfect. Woken at 3.30 on a cold morning, he struggled into every piece of warm underwear he could find before putting on his uniform. Lighting a cigarette, he scrambled onto the aircrew van with the others. After the briefing, the crew assembled in the operational canteen. Never one to be put off his food, Wlad started on his bacon and eggs as he sat opposite Ladro. Ladro talked to the wireless operator next to him. Wlad half listened to the conversation as he ate.

'Well,' said Ladro, 'I wonder if we'll see any of these fighters we've heard so much about.'

'I hope not, sir,' replied the wireless operator.

'Just the same,' said Ladro, looking around the table, 'we'd better keep our eyes open today.'

'That's about all we can do,' Andrew, the rear gunner, muttered.

'What's that? Speak up, man,' said Ladro.

Andrew reddened, but repeated his remark. 'I mean, how can these old crates fight off anything more than a Tiger Moth?' he added.

Ladro pulled out his pipe, watching Andrew closely. 'That's the way to defeat, Andrew. Men count more than weapons.'

Andrew shrugged.

'We either win or lose, but attitude has a great deal of influence on the final outcome,' said Ladro emphatically.

'It's more like live or die,' said the navigator.

'Not necessarily,' replied Ladro. 'Everyone is too scared of dying.'

'Not just now, sir, please. I'm still eating. All this talk is bad for my digestion,' said Wlad as he mopped up his eggs with a slice of bread. He lit a cigarette, and eyed the other men. The conversation had jarred with them.

In the van they sat in morose silence. The heavy parachute bags were heaved off at the dispersal point, and the crew took up their stations in the aircraft without any further talk.

Entering the front turret was something of a struggle for a big man like Wlad. Fully dressed in fur-lined trousers, jacket and flying boots, he needed assistance. He hated this part of the flight. He would inevitably end up sweating, then would spend the rest of the flight in the draughty turret being chilled by the wind, resulting in cramps and bouts of colds. However, he had no qualms about entering the turret before take-off, nor did he worry about weather conditions during the take-off. Ladro had not been known to misjudge anything. The rest was in the hands of fate, he thought.

Now, with the double door closed firmly by the second pilot, he waited, impatient to be in the air. At last the engines came to

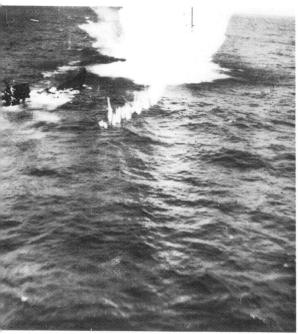

(*Left*) U-boat under attack by RAF aircraft. (*Right*) Our wireless operator, E. Siadecki (killed over the Bay); Davidstow Moor

U-boat on the surface.

(*Left*) Our navigator, Sergeant Streng, by a Mk XIV Wellington at RAF Chivenor, 1944.

(*Below*) Wellington GR XIVs of 304 (Polish) Squadron, 1945.

life, and they were moving away from the dispersal point. The time was 4.50 a.m. It was still completely dark outside. Fine, cold drizzle settled on the turret. They taxied slowly around the aerodrome, then, with the engines roaring, took off into the darkness.

Three hours later, and Wlad was lighting another cigarette. They were closing on the Spanish coast. The sky was now blue and cloudless, the sea smooth. Wlad scanned the horizon, the sky and the sea ceaselessly. A slight change in the horizon would tell an experienced air gunner that land lay ahead.

They turned on 280° and flew parallel to the coast, maintaining a distance of roughly five miles from the land. At 11.00 a.m. they changed the course to 070°, and were homeward bound at last. 6½ hours had passed, with 3½ left. Ahead, the pale horizon merged with the sea without a trace of separation. The engines droned steadily.

'Aircraft, seven o'clock, low,' came Andrew's voice from the rear turret. 'Unable to identify as yet.'

Silence on the intercom. Wlad froze.

'Two of them. No, three. Another now.' Andrew's tone of voice changed.

What seemed like hours passed before he spoke again:

'Fighters.'

He left his mike on, and they could all hear his rapid breathing.

'Well?' said Ladro sharply.

'They're Jerries,' Andrew mumbled.

'Out with it.' Ladro's voice was taut.

'Four Ju88s, eight o'clock, low, approaching, three miles.'

'Right. Jettisoning the depth charges,' said Ladro. The aircraft began to dive.

'Two miles, approaching.'

'Wlad, Andrew; get ready.' Ladro's voice was unemotional. 'Depth charges jettisoned.'

Wlad came to life. He swivelled the turret, adjusted the sight. He felt neither panic nor despair. They would fight to the end, he knew that much.

113

'Navigator, pass the position to the wireless operator. Tell him to have the OA message ready.'

'One mile,' said Andrew. 'Six o'clock, our height, in line astern. Turning; definitely Ju88s.'

Ladro made a sharp, steep turn. Wlad saw the fighters come out from under the wing. They also were in a steep turn, one following the other. Their dark silhouettes were unmistakable.

'Wireless operator,' said Ladro. He cleared his throat.

'Yes, sir.'

'Stand by with the OA message.'

'800 yards,' said Wlad, adjusting his guns.

The leading Junkers tightened his turn until the two aircraft faced one another. He levelled out, and flew straight at them.

'Ready, Wlad?'

'Ready.'

'Wireless operator, send the message. Wlad, fire in bursts. Now.'

Instantly the multi-coloured tracers shot through the space between the planes. Wlad's hands felt sweaty and clumsy. He sighted the guns again, and pressed the fire button. The battle was under way.

The Wellington side-slipped towards the sea, shuddering from Wlad's fire. He felt the aircraft jolt slightly.

'Hit on port wing,' said the second pilot.

The second Ju88 did not fire. The enemy turned and climbed steeply. Engines thundered. The Wellington levelled out just feet above the sea. Wlad saw the last Junkers diving towards them. Ladro threw the aircraft into a climbing turn to port.

Wlad opened fire, and so did the Junkers. Bullets splashed across the water towards them. Ladro swung the aircraft violently to starboard. They had not been hit. The first attack was over.

Ladro pulled the aircraft up to 200 or 300 feet. They waited for the next attack.

'Coming in from three o'clock,' said the second pilot. Ladro rapidly shut the port engine and pushed the left rudder. The aircraft swung to port. The leading Junkers fired, but missed. His wingman pressed home his attack in spite of fire from the Wellington. Again Ladro side-slipped, but the aircraft shuddered. Smoke filled the plane.

'Hit acrosss the fuselage,' said the navigator.

'Watch out from the sun,' shouted the wireless operator.

Ladro could see nothing, blinded by the sun. He corkscrewed the aircraft, dodging the invisible enemy. For a fraction of a second, Wlad had a glimpse of water boiling under the hail of bullets.

Ladro tightened the turn so that the wing tip almost touched the water. Again, tense moments as the plane shook from the enemy bullets. Suddenly, an agonising blow knocked Wlad sideways against the turret.

'Bastards,' he heard himself shouting. 'I've been hit.' Almost at once the strength ebbed out of him. He was aware of warm fluid coursing down his chest and back. Somewhere, what seemed like an immense distance away, the rest of the crew was jabbering excitedly over the intercom.

'They're coming in twos.' He could make out Andrew's voice.

'Wireless operator, see Wlad,' said Ladro. But no one came.

Time after time Wlad was thrown painfully against the projections in the turret. At one stage he saw two Junkers coming in at sea level while the other two circled above them. The aircraft was thrown again in violent evasive action, causing Wlad to shout in pain. He saw tracers streaming in from the blue sky, accelerating, curving towards them.

'Starboard down,' shouted Andrew. The aircraft heaved crazily, shuddered from Andrew's gunfire and bullets from the Junkers. The voices stopped; the intercom was gone.

The engines roared. Pain swept over Wlad as the aircraft continued twisting, turning, diving, climbing. He could no longer follow the fight, gradually losing consciousness as he lost more blood.

Wlad was not to know until much later that once his guns were out of order, the Junkers made a determined effort to press the attack from the front. They were intent on hitting the pilot next.

Ladro banked the aircraft into a side-slip and turn a fraction of a second before the leading Ju88 opened fire, missed, and dived over their heads. Following that, the plane was thrown into an almost continuous series of turns at sea level. It trembled from the fire from the rear gun. The engines suddenly went silent, then roared up again. At times the enemy was so close that the details of their camouflage were clearly visible.

Then there were only three Junkers. One suddenly turned and flew east, trailing black smoke behind him. This obviously came as some surprise to the Germans, who did not take to suffering casualties at the hands of an unwieldy twin-engined aircraft which should have been shot down a long time ago. They attacked repeatedly in open vic formation, sending an avalanche of metal into the Wellington. The second pilot was hit and collapsed to the floor, seriously wounded. Andrew ran out of ammunition.

From that moment it was all up to Ladro. The Junkers came in once, twice, then formed a close vic and came head on at the Wellington. No shot was fired. The Ju88s grew in size. Still they came, until Ladro could see their faces in the cockpits. Someone shook a fist. Nearer and nearer they came, finally filling the whole front view. Ladro heard their thundering engines. In a flash they were gone, leaving the Wellington rocking in their slipstreams. Ladro banked the aircraft, and they watched the three Junkers in close formation turn towards France and disappear over the horizon.

The time was exactly midday. One of the longest air battles of the war, lasting 58 minutes, was over. Ladro set course for England.

After a long struggle they managed to open the front turret. Wlad was unconscious, but later recalled coming to at intervals.

Later, Ladro admitted that by the end of the fight he was so totally drained that he barely understood what was happening. To the questions of the crew he merely nodded his head, letting them use their own initiative to do the necessary tasks.

Nearly three hours later the English coast appeared. Ladro

flew on until he came to Predannack.

Having secured the wounded, Ladro fired red flares, descended in a turn, cut the magneto switches off and crash landed along the runway in use. There was no fire.

Wlad came to in hospital. Both he and the second pilot took some time to recover from their wounds. Wlad returned to the squadron, but the second pilot was grounded, and eventually invalided out of the Air Force. By the time Wlad resumed flying, his crew had completed its operational tour and dispersed.

Not long after, Ladro joined the OTU at Silloth as Squadron Leader In Charge of Flying.

*

Now he sat behind his desk with a pipe in his hand. He looked at me for some time. He was of medium height, pale, with the pale blue eyes of the classic RAF pilot of the day. He looked calm, controlled, reflective.

'So, Mr Jaworski, we're here because we're devoted to flying.' Embarrassed by such an unusual opening, I blushed and mumbled something. Ladro then began talking about what was involved in being a captain rather than just a pilot. This and subsequent talks of his, almost always on a one to one basis, sounded reasonable and well thought out. Coming from him, one felt that what he said was backed by hard-gained experience. I certainly never faltered in my admiration for him, as well as his deeds.

We pilots now started on dual flying in the Wellingtons. This was my first experience of qualified Polish instructors. I had done over six hundred hours of flying by then, but the instructors had all had at least one operational tour in Bomber Command. Here, unlike the English approach where one flew solo after a minimum of instruction and did one's best, the instructors sat stolidly, patiently correcting minutiae until they were absolutely satisfied. Even then they let one on a solo with a resigned shrug and air of misgiving. It took me two hours and forty minutes to go solo, but Poles paid no attention to this aspect of instructing.

117

It was a relief to have Ladro personally take over some of the difficult if not dangerous aspects of teaching us to fly the aircraft. He instructed us how to do single engine flying and landing, including landing without flaps. We went through the circuits and bumps routine on all the types of Wellington available.

At last we were joined by our crews. The first flights – practising air to air firing, bombing, and radar practice were almost painfully hard. Everyone was nervous and self-conscious, everyone that is except Nikel. Although by nature he was too easygoing to be thorough in his flying, his humour was of vital importance to us.

From then on the pace of flying began to accelerate. We were down for a series of long navigational flights. Before that, one of the gunnery instructors wanted to check out the progress in air to air flying made by our gunners. It was to be a routine two-hour flight.

CHAPTER EIGHT

Out of my Depth

We took off for the flight in unpromising weather. A gusting westerly, a pale blue sky with a fringe of dark clouds sitting tightly on the horizon. Take-off was along the shortest runway, straight over the town. The wind blew across the runway, and the aircraft was tricky even to taxi. I had a fierce battle with the aircraft trying to keep it on the runway during the take-off, then in keeping it climbing at a safe speed and away from the various high buildings in the town, not to mention those in the aerodrome. The air was so rough that the instructor called off the exercise even before we reached the range. The wireless operator told us that there had been an urgent recall to all OTU aircraft. Alternatively we could land at the nearest aerodrome. By then we were flying into a force nine gale. Nikel's expressive face looked as I felt: we should never have been allowed up. It was too late for recalls now.

We were the last aircraft in the sky by the time we reached the airfield. Buffeted, I circled around a few times, saw the wind sock nearly horizontal, swinging around in the gusts. We were in trouble. I watched the last aircraft landing, saw it cartwheel in a crash. The sight of that certainly did nothing to boost my self-confidence. Reluctantly I went through the landing drill and wrestled with the aircraft towards the runway, trying to ignore the problems. I touched the ground, and immediately a gust lifted us back into the air. I pushed the throttles fully forward to save us from a crash. At a price. At the low overshoot speed we were drifting towards the hangars. Just made it. I had a glimpse of upturned faces, of people running out of the hangars. Then the church spire came at us. Missing that also, we began to gather enough speed to climb for another circuit and approach, more nervously this time. Another brief touch-down. This time the gust threw us up and sideways, knocking us off the runway. On full throttle we seemed to be standing still. Then, agonisingly slowly, we crept crabwise past the same hangars, the engines roaring on full power at temperatures well over permissible.

By the time we climbed up the whole crew was in a panic. We circled, smoked cigarettes. We checked the weather conditions around Silloth. All aerodromes were closed: gale force winds, low cloud, rain, no visibility. That was coming here unless we landed quickly.

I was on my own, up against it. But by then I was past feeling panicky. A hard lesson in the realities of survival had descended upon me, as always, so unfairly. I simply did not know how to handle the aircraft under such extreme conditions. Nothing I did know worked. No aircraft I had ever flown had such large vertical surfaces and was so sensitive to high winds close to the ground. However, land I must.

I made my plans looking with loathing at the runway, which at best was short and hemmed in by a fence and the proximity of the town. I changed tactics, and made a long approach, cautiously coming in low and fast with lots of engine power and the flaps only partly down. I let the aircraft turn into the wind to fly almost sideways. At the last minute I forced the aircraft to line up, kept the engines going; we touched down, not badly. I watched the end of the runway approaching fast. Suddenly I shut the engines and applied the brakes, and swung the aircraft across the grass into the wind and onto the tarmac. We were safe.

When I cut the engines I heard the roar of the gale. My mouth was dry. I said nothing to the ground crew, simply wrote on the form 700 'heavy landing.'

I found out later that practically the whole aerodrome was watching my antics, first attracted by the crashing plane, then scampering from the hangars. Ladro said nothing. In the time available, given the war conditions, one could teach a pilot just so much. The rest was up to the pilot, and when faced with extreme conditions, his luck.

120

The flying continued, the pace stepped up. We did a navigational flight of six hours and thirty minutes, then a number of night flights, each longer than the previous one. Ladro came with us twice on night cross-country flights. Cross-country is a misnomer because we flew above the sea, towards the Outer Hebrides or the western Irish coast. The first time Ladro came with us we were forced to return due to bad weather after just over two hours' flying. He left me to make the decision, and made no comment. On the other hand, he spent much of his time prowling around the aircraft watching the activities of the crew. Nikel for one could hardly hide his dislike of Ladro or his presence in the aircraft; he felt that Ladro disturbed the little routines that the crew was setting up for itself, and made the crew feel uneasy by his unspoken criticism.

＊

I felt the need for city crowds. The crew dispersed into different parts of the country. Nikel inevitably travelled up to see his fiancée in Blackpool, Wrobel had some different undefined attachment in Leeds, and so on. But for the few thousand who travelled on the train, I went on my own to London.

In London I decided to stay in one of the Polish clubs – the White Eagle. By then the build-up for the invasion of Europe had begun. The American army was pouring into Britain. As always, London reflected the current military and political changes. Now uniforms proliferated, with the Americans dominating the scene.

The club, located in the Belgrave Square area, was formerly a residential hotel. Now it had lost a great deal of its former elegance. The sleeping accommodation was somewhat spartan, the facilities crowded. Among the elderly military and civilian emigrés there was a considerable number of young men in uniforms of all services, some highly decorated, some familiar because of their exposure in the news. There were also a few Polish women, mainly on the staff, working as volunteers in various capacities.

121

The first day of my stay in the club I went to the cashier's desk to pay for my coffee. I saw the desk was run by a young woman; fair-haired, rather thin-faced and pale, made up and dressed in the city style. She handed me my change, talking all the time to a young army officer standing near her. She spoke rapidly, in an animated tone of voice. Rather nervously too, I thought to myself. Then she glanced at me.

'Josek?' Her expressive face went through a range of emotions. 'Josek.' I stood stunned. She rose, moved swiftly to me and embraced me impulsively. Momentarily the scent of her perfume and warmth enveloped me. Holding my hand, she moved back a little.

'Well, Josek, can you still not recognise me?' I did. She was the daughter of a High School headmaster. I had met her in Paris, and before that in Hungary. And even before then. Two and a half years ago, being a year younger than me, she had looked rather different. But even then her high spirits and promise of good looks had been evident.

Still not letting go of my hand, she glanced at my RAF pilot's badge.

'Well, you don't have to behave like a cool Englishman with me, Josek. I know what you're really like.' I glanced at the army lieutenant. I was blushing with embarrassment and confusion. Not unnaturally, he looked far from pleased, and would no doubt have happily ditched me in a distant sea.

Immediately there was the question of my name. I was not Josek but Geniek, which is how I had registered myself at the club. I had little doubt that she would ferret something out, being an inquisitive type. Five minutes later she marshalled me into a corner carrying a glass of 'continental' tea, while I managed to procure a real drink for myself. Aniela, as I will call her, was attractive, and at the time an extremely rare sort of person – a young Polish woman. She moved her chair close to mine, and sniffed at the whisky.

'Honestly, you are the image of the English pilot,' she said, disrespectfully, I thought.

'What do you expect me to do? Drink wodka and dance

Mazowsze?' I answered, annoyed by the remark.

She laughed. 'We're not from Mazowsze, and let's have a bit less of the cool. Tell me, what are you up to?'

I did not have time to reply. There was a great deal of chair shuffling around us, and a lot of chattering, some of it addressed to Aniela.

'Let's go for a walk,' she said suddenly. 'You're not paying any attention to me.' I did not really understand, but dutifully followed her out.

There were many things to be said, no doubt about it. For myself, my exchange of names with Geniek had to be explained. I examined Aniela critically. She certainly was eye-catching, but seemed awfully thin and underdeveloped. I thought she could do with a couple of inches on her bust to begin with . . .

'Josek,' she said, looking me straight in the eye. I blushed again, and turned away.

It was not a spectacular evening as far as the weather went. I wanted to sit down somewhere. I told Aniela a little of my escapes from Hungary and France. Encouraged by her attention, I explained the name swop with Geniek. To my surprise she did not react.

'You were always mad about flying, so it's not really a surprise. Anyway, you've been lucky to find yourself such a helpful friend.'

The conversation began to lag. I was never a 'ladies' man', neither by nature nor by practice. And going out with an English girl was a totally different experience. Aniela did not volunteer any information, and I was at a loss over what to ask her. At last I suggested that we stop at a pub for a drink.

Aniela laughed. 'God help me, Josek, Geniek – whatever you want to call yourself. Are you really so thoroughly Anglicised?'

'I don't know what you mean.'

'You ought to remember that it is not good manners for a Polish girl to go into places like that.'

I was needled. 'Pubs aren't just for prostitutes, you know.'

She started to giggle, then controlled herself. We made our way back, and she went home.

We met the next day in the club. That morning there were the inevitable uniforms surrounding her. Aniela introduced me as an old friend, and left it at that. On the whole I was scanned as a possible rival and, unfortunately for my ego, was quickly dismissed. Perhaps deservedly so . . .

I could not make my mind up about Aniela. On the occasions that I went for walks around London, staring at the bombed sites, I tried not to think too hard about her, and one or two other topics. I would return to the club to hear Aniela's clear voice and laughter. She scandalised the older members of the club. We went to shows and cinemas in a group, and if we touched it was by accident.

The day of my departure came. Aniela told me that she was working in a Polish Government office, but did not say where or what she was doing. And who dared to ask or say too much in those days?

Aniela accompanied me to the railway station.

'Please write,' she said, suddenly tremendously serious. 'We haven't really talked, you know.'

'I know. I'll write,' I said, and left.

*

Bleary-eyed from the all night journey, I surveyed the bleak scene: Predannack, not an untypical Cornish aerodrome of Coastal Command. The ground flat, the sea but a few hundred yards away. From experience I knew of the vertical coastal rocks, several hundred feet high, right there at the end of the runway. The cold wind was merciless that morning. Once again Coastal Command had lived up to its reputation in the location of its aerodromes. Presently I was taken to the living quarters, then to the sergeants' mess for breakfast.

I was early, and few aircrew were yet in sight. Here the aircrew issue of fur-lined jackets, thick white sweaters and fleece-lined boots proved to be particularly important, as the heating was far from adequate. I sat down to the breakfast with an air gunner I knew, who told me what was currently happening in the squadron.

Korbut was now a squadron commander, a popular one it seemed. Already this month there had been two night attacks on U-boats. However, two crews had disappeared without trace on flights over the Bay. Fighters were as active as ever, if not more so. And a pilot had killed a ditched crew.

'He what?' I asked, shocked by the blandness of such a statement. The gunner looked grim. Apparently, while returning from a night flight, the radar operator had located a dinghy in a position less than fifteen miles from the French coast.

For us, that distance was very close to the enemy. Not only radar but numerous German observation posts could, and were known to, detect the patrolling British aircraft. Once located, the Luftwaffe could scramble its single engine fighters within minutes and dispatch the luckless aircraft. The pilot at first refused to take the routine action; he was expected to climb over the dinghy to a sufficient height to send a radio signal. In the process he would of course break the radio silence, allowing all and sundry to take a fix on his own position. In the event, after a heated argument, they flew for ten minutes west then broke the radio silence, signalling the sighting and position. Then, arguing hard as they flew back, they failed to intercept the instructions which the Group sent them, and failed to find the dinghy again. The crew returned, implacably split up.

Korbut broke the crew up and re-formed it. It was given a new second pilot and various odd people. Then, in spite of the heat generated by the incident, Korbut packed them off on operational flying immediately.

The ditched crew was never found.

'Maybe they were picked up,' I suggested. The gunner shrugged and said nothing. It seemed that my remark was not that well timed. I was just another . . . pilot.

'Well, excuse me, I've got to . . .' I left the gunner's company.

I walked restlessly around the mess, greeting people I had known, looking out over the aerodrome at the white Mk XIV's, checking the wind sock, examining the sky. I felt like I was more involved than ever before.

The whole crew arrived that day, fatigued and rather uncertain of themselves. Even Nikel looked apprehensive. At lunchtime I saw Wacek. He looked paler and more fragile. He was still wearing the inevitable bicycle clips, though to my knowledge he had never owned a bike. Like Geniek, he wore his cap over his left eye. His face creased in the too-ready smile.

'Well, well, Geniek. Good to see you again.' He put his arm around me and led me to the bar. Then I took him over to introduce him to the crew. Wacek beamed as insincerely as ever, bowed, shook hands, praised everyone. At last we went back for another drink.

'Jesus Christ, Geniek,' he said. 'I sent you to get yourself a crew.'

'Well?' I said, defiantly. He shook his head and looked away, obviously disappointed.

'Perhaps it's not your fault,' he sighed. 'After all, what can you expect if they're bringing them from Siberia to become aircrew?' Wacek was alluding to the massive influx of Poles into the forces in the West, men who been released from Russia under an agreement after the Russian-German war had broken out. I was not really offended. I knew that he was concerned for me. We did form a rather motley crew, no one physically robust or projecting an aggressive image. We did not even have an officer who could help by pulling rank on some particularly awkward administrator if we happened to land in any RAF stations.

'Oh, well, come on. Let's see the Major.' The Major, holding a cigarette in his silver holder, was pleased to see me. He offered me one of his special cigarettes with the gold band from his case. I refused. He had somehow had these cigarettes brought out of an obscure part of the world where someone still held a store of Polish cigarettes. We shook hands, and I introduced my crew, who shuffled past. Then we stood still.

'Splendid, splendid,' said the Major. 'Well, there you are then, Geniek. A crew of your own at last. You'll all do great things, I'm certain of that.'

Wacek and I accompanied the Major to his quarters. We drank the proffered coffee while the Major spoke of the current Polish situation.

'The West owes us a great debt. Once again we have saved them from total defeat. And the USA, with ten million Americans of Polish origin . . . I have great faith . . .' He was a good man. Perhaps time had taken a sudden and very long leap, or perhaps he simply preferred not to think in any other way.

The next day we paraded before the Wing Commander. He was brisk and complimentary, but I thought I detected a trace of a smile as he looked us over.

'You know what is expected,' he said, addressing me. 'You've been through the whole of the training.'

And once again I started the tedious and unending training. First, the familiarisation flights, followed then by radar training. I was devastated to discover how bad we were as a crew. We simply could not synchronise our activities in simulated attacks on U-boats in an acceptable fashion. More long hours in the air would follow before we were ready for operational flying.

One day Taubert, our navigator, took me aside. 'Sorry, skip, bad news. I'm going to the hospital for a check-up. Something seems to be blocking me here.' He pointed to his stomach. I was annoyed. What a time to be sick.

The next day the hospital telephoned. Sergeant Taubert was going for an immediate operation. We went to see him. After the visit, the nurse called me over.

'I'm sorry to tell you that your navigator has cancer of the stomach.' I stared at her uncomprehendingly. She shook her head. 'It's incurable, you know.' And so, poor Taubert, at the ripe age of twenty-six, disappeared from us forever.

When we started to pick up the nitty gritty of day to day life again, we realised that we were in serious trouble. There were simply no spare navigators.

I saw Wacek. 'We'll see what we can do,' he said. At first I went for a few training flights with my old crew, and admired again Wacek's excellence in low level bombing. With Wacek's intervention people soon began to help out. Presently a more senior navigator, Flying Officer Kawa, started to fly with us. Even the Major gave us a hand on occasions.

CHAPTER NINE
Captain of Crew

In March 1944, without forewarning, the squadron moved again, this time to RAF Chivenor in North Devon. For the first time we found ourselves in a Coastal Command station close to an attractive market town, Barnstaple. The aerodrome itself was located nearer to the sea, with a long south/north runway. The station had been built early on in the war, and the key buildings were within reasonable walking distance from each other. No sooner had we arrived when Flight Lieutenant Ochalski asked me to fly an operation with his crew, as second pilot. I was glad to do so, especially as my wireless operator was to come with us, and would thus have a chance to do his first operation.

Ochalski was a tall, well-built man, in his late twenties. He was very self-confident. I watched him push the throttles forward without hesitation or subtlety. With the overload, we lumbered along for a long time until Ochalski impatiently heaved the aircraft off the ground. Not my style, but we were in safe hands. So we took off into the night on the familiar Bay of Biscay patrol.

The Battle of the Atlantic carried on unabated. Most Coastal Command squadrons saw a lot of action against U-Boats, particularly in the Bay area. Our crews had attacked repeatedly recently, and had brought back some classic photographs of the encounters. Some of the attacks were carried out much closer to the French coast than any margin of safety allowed, but at that time it hardly seemed to matter.

That night we had no such luck, although we checked out a

(*Left*) Before an operational flight, probably at Chivenor in 1944. (*Right*) Our wireless operator, gunner and radar operator in front of a Polish 304 Squadron – 1944.

A Wellington Mk XIV at Chivenor.

TO* 304 Sqd. CHIVENOR.					
FROM* 61 O.T.U.	Originator's Number P 240	Date 28/4	Your/My	Number and Date	

(Write horizontally) Please inform Mr. E. JAWORSKI
believed to be on your squadron that
his friend Sgt. Jozef Jaworzyn
(YM 660) lost his life yesterday
Thursday 27th April 1944 as the
result of an aircraft accident

No. 304 (POLISH) SQUADRON
1 MAY 1944
R.A.F.

The news of Geniek's death, under his assumed identity.

The top photograph shows the author's crew at Benbecula, except for
Sergeant Puchlik. The bottom photograph shows the inside of an Aircrew Mess.

large number of radar contacts. Again I saw the Spanish coast and its lights, watched cars with full headlights. We all observed these sights with a prim disapproval. How dare they . . . Then on course, due north into the darkness. Finally, saturated with coffee and cigarettes, I watched the pale dawn on the eastern horizon. Ochalski alerted the crew, checking each one individually. The rear gunner came out of his trance, the navigator attentive in the astrodome. At that moment the sky was full of low level stratus clouds, perfect traps for the unwary. I scanned the eastern horizon repeatedly. The microphone crackled; the radar operator:

'Four, three o'clock, very close.' At once Ochalski threw the aircraft into a steep turn to starboard; I saw the tracers coming out of the semi-darkness, curving slowly in our direction, accelerating. I pulled the intercom plug out and made towards the front machine gun. The aircraft trembled as Ochalski pushed the throttles fully forward. I practically fell onto the machine gun, my hands sweating so much that I could hardly maintain a grip on it. Our rear guns were firing in long bursts, the engines roared, and Ochalski threw the aircraft into unbelievable side slipping turns. Tracers criss-crossed the space around us. Nobody spoke, or so I thought, until I realised that I was not plugged into the intercom. Suddenly we were in a cloud, God knows in what flying position. Out for a moment; more tracers, back into the cloud, terribly slowly. I felt horribly vulnerable. I calculated that Ochalski was turning the aircraft on a course for home, on full power. I stayed at the gun. Presently we were out of the clouds in the full daylight.

Ochalski had not allowed the wireless operator to send the usual message. Was that an incredible oversight or did it stem from over-confidence? It turned out to have been a calculated risk in order not to give our position away before we had time to reach the range of our own fighters.

As I made my way past him, Ochalski gave me a crooked grin. His face was covered with sweat. I went on to the fuselage, where the smell of cordite was very strong, and all kinds of navigational gear – charts and maps, papers – were floating everywhere. The navigator looked shaken, but we must all have been on our nerve edges as well as tired out.

We flew straight for Predannack and landed on the last of our petrol after nearly eleven hours. We refuelled and flew back to the base.

For Ochalski it was to be just a prelude; in April of the same year he was to be involved in a full length battle with Ju88 long range fighters. He survived the fight untouched, although the aircraft was badly damaged, and nearly all the outer crew members were wounded.

Meanwhile, Wartan arrived at the squadron. After some scheming we put together a crew with Wartan as my second pilot, with his gunner and navigator making up the rest of the crew. Off we went on our first operation, on a dark night. Chivenor was an excellent aerodrome if the wind blew from the sea on a night of an operational flight. I happened to be in luck that night, and my first take-off as captain of the crew went as smoothly as was possible under the circumstances.

After about an hour I let Wartan take over, and walked into the back of the aircraft feeling vaguely uneasy. Could Wartan cope if . . .? At 500 feet, on a moonless night? I sat down on the step and lit a cigarette. A tremor unexpectedly passed through the aircraft. I stood up, suddenly alert. We had flown into low level rain clouds, in which we had to stay for a few hours. After some time the wireless operator was on the intercom.

'Immediate recall by the Group,' he said. 'All aircraft,' he added, as if reading my thoughts. By then we were flying into rapidly increasing disturbances. We turned back, only to find that by then the bad weather had also reached the coast. The Group had saved me from indecision by diverting us to Davidstow Moor. Because of its elevation, the aerodrome still had some visibility. We landed while heavy rain was sweeping the runway. Seven hours, only a short flight, but the crew seemed pleased.

Back we went to days and nights of radar, low level bombing and navigational exercises, culminating in the flight on the Viking exercise. This was a training attack on one of our submarines.

Operational secrecy demanded that the exact location would not be disclosed. On a perfect night, complete with full moon, we flew north to the Irish Sea, and at a given point began a radar search. Having found her on the radar, we finally spotted the wake of the tiny vessel on the mirror-smooth sea. It was a memorable scene, with the moon shining on the innocuous looking sub. We exchanged colours of the day with its escort, made a few coordinated full scale attacks and returned to base some six hours later. After this exercise we were operational again.

We flew two operations, to be recalled each time after meeting different variations of bad weather. Both flights lasted around nine hours. I do not think that we consciously graded the weather conditions – or surmised how much danger was posed by any particular condition, or what our chances of survival would be – because landing in the fog or rain, flying in minimal visibility and taking such risks were simply part of the operational requirements which we needed to be able to cope with, as with any other problems we might run into.

Training continued relentlessly. Korbut was determined to keep the squadron at top level performance, and while we understood his wish we were hardly enthusiastic over the endless radar and bombing exercises. Our next operation saw our third successive recall by the Group. This time they seemed to have gambled too much. By the time we had reached the Scilly Islands the whole of Devon and Cornwall was under low cloud and all the aerodromes closed. We diverted from one place to another, only to be refused permission to land with visibility close to zero. Finally I took the aircraft to 2,500 feet.

Long-range bombers may fly at 15,000 or 25,000 feet, but to me 2,500 feet seemed a height that one climbed to only when in trouble. Above us shone the full moon and stars, but below us there was nothing but uninterrupted white cotton-like layers of cloud, hugging the ground closely. Nikel and the rest of the crew checked their parachutes.

'How are we doing?' I asked Kawa.

'Nothing so far', was the reply. 'The Group gave us a course

045 while they're checking out possible landing places. North Yorkshire was mentioned . . .'

'Jesus,' Nikel said. 'We're still only over Devon.'

I turned the aircraft on course without much conviction, climbing slowly up to 3,500 feet, then setting the engines on the most economical speed. I had never jumped from an aircraft, and this would have to be done in cold blood, so to speak. I began to recheck the course against the compass, a nervous and rather meaningless activity. We droned on.

'The Group recommends that we try Valley,' said the wireless operator.

'Recommends?'

'Well, yes. It seems that the visibility is practically nil, but they have some kind of flame-throwing flare path.' We were not amused. I had heard of a new idea for landing in fog called FIDO (Fog Investigation and Dispersal Operation), but had no notion of whether it had actually been put into practice.

'What's the alternative?'

'Silloth.'

'That's two more hours.'

'Weather's closing down over the whole country', said Kawa. I asked for the course for Valley.

'320, safety height 4,800 feet.' We changed course and began to climb.

After a time the radar operator identified the coast, and we corrected courses. I began to descend uneasily, aware of the proximity of the mountains. Total darkness surrounded us.

'We must be practically over the aerodrome', said the navigator. I kept the aircraft in a steep descending turn, then had a glimpse of a light at 1,200 feet. The aerodrome had powerful boundary lights which were just visible through the fog. At last we came to FIDO. First there was a series of yellow fog-penetrating flames which led towards the runway. Four of these flames were grouped at a point where one should have been lined up for the final approach. I was at 500 feet when a colossal thermal nearly turned the aircraft over. The turbulence remained with us all the way in; it was, as someone said, like 'flying through the gates of hell'. Simultaneously came the lines of yellow flames marking the runway, the turbulence in the air, our bumping and heaving, suddenly remembering that with all the flames around we were carrying our full bomb load. Then we were down safely, and as we were taxiing towards the control tower we saw the space in front of it packed with aircraft. It seemed that every aircraft above the UK had made for Valley.

For Kawa it was the last operational flight of his tour. I doubt whether he was sorry about it.

*

By the next morning the weather had cleared up enough to allow us to return to base.

It seemed as though there would never be an end to the training. On many occasions the flying exceeded eight hours per day. Thankfully the time for another leave was coming up. At the last moment I was asked to do an operation with a senior crew who had only just been in the national news after a spectacular night fight with two Me 110s. The rear gunner had shot one down; the wreckage was there for all to see, floating close to the English coast. As a result the gunner was recommended for an immediate DFM. On this operation the first pilot could not fly, so the crew asked me to come with them. I was flattered, and accepted eagerly.

At the briefing, when the routes were displayed, I felt a wave of dismay from the crew. We had been given a track that was as close to the French coast as anyone from the squadron had been assigned to; but then, were the crew not one of the best?

The night was dark and moonless. We were due to take off late in order to arrive at, and stay close to, the French coast throughout the night, and then depart at dawn along a circuitous route. At the operational canteen I found the crew agitated, riding on an adrenaline flow. We all registered the preflight tension in our own fashion, the signs being fairly easy to read in the others.

The night was still, the take-off direction towards Barnstaple.

133

As I performed the cockpit drill my hands were sweating. I pushed the throttles forward, the aircraft taking its time to accelerate. The red lights marking the end of the runway were in front of us before I pulled her off the ground. Finally we turned over the village, dodging the hill tops. At 500 feet I started to turn the aircraft on course.

'170°', said the navigator.

We were now on course for the Channel and the French coast. The crew was tense and irritable, snapping out the usual drill. The night stayed pitch black. I fought off the urge to reduce the height. The coast was close now, we must have been spotted by the enemy by now, their radar checking out our progress. In the aircraft there were waves of chatter between the radar operator, the navigator and the wireless operator over the radar blips and their positions.

Hours passed. Sometime close to 03.00 hours the radar operator spoke up.

'U-boat, twenty-one miles, 10° starboard.' His voice carried no doubt.

There was a rush of activity. We would hold back the breaking of the radio silence for a few more minutes. The French coast was clear on the radar.

'Eighteen miles on course, U-boat still on the surface. There is an aircraft escort with it.' A pause, but before we had time to take stock he said;

'There is another aircraft there, must be attacking it.' The wireless operator confirmed that there was an attack by an RAF aircraft taking place. By that time we could see the battle – flashes of guns, tracers.

'The aircraft reports serious damage; returning to base immediately.'

'Seven miles on course,' said the radar operator. I began to sweat, and started to reduce height.

'Stand by for attack', I said.

The second pilot moved off to the front.

'Stand by to lower the Leigh Light. Lower it now.' 300 feet.

'Course 270 after the attack.'

'U-boat two miles, enemy fighters approaching rapidly.' 150 feet.

'One mile, on course, fighters closing in.'

'Bomb door open.'

'Fighters attacking from port and starboard.' Excited voices. Fifty feet.

'Leigh Light on.'

Everything happening at once. A flash of powerful light dazzled me. Fifty feet, bomb door open, I saw nothing, blinded by a flare from the U-boat. Fighters attacking.

'Evasive action.' I counted to ten, ignoring the voices, then dropped the bombs and pulled the bomb door lever up.

'Leigh Light up.' I tried to turn the aircraft slowly, gently pushing the throttles forward. A single hasty move now and we would be in the water in two and a half seconds. Outside in the darkness I could see the tracers moving in our direction. Our rear gunner was firing in long bursts at one aircraft, now the other, trying to keep them away while we were in this vulnerable position. Finally I was able to open the throttles fully and start to turn.

'Attacking again. Turn, turn.' Tracers again, a furious exchange of fire.

'The U-boat's still there,' said the radar operator.

The attacks continued while we flew at top speed in a westerly direction, twisting and turning. Single engine fighters were not supposed to be so keen to follow, yet the tracers seemed to be as vicious as ever.

'We've been hit again,' said the navigator.

Time seemed suspended before the radar operator saw the fighters turning back. Day was coming in now rapidly. The crew was silent. We changed courses several times, and in full daylight, on a cloudless morning turned towards the Scilly Isles. Fatigue was now settling in, and the fuel supply was low after such heavy use. The damage to the fuselage and the wing did not look serious.

By then the crew was not displeased, but I did not feel too happy. The Jerries had tricked us; by now the U-boat could be safe in the harbour.

The flight had lasted just ten hours. During the debriefing the crew took over. I listened for a while as they refought the attack, then left.

In the evening I boarded the train for London, off on my leave for a week.

*

Once I began to search for a navigator, or looked for ways of 'hiring' the crew out, I was soon forced to appreciate the complexities of the squadron's aircrew manning levels. A full complement of twenty-four crews meant that there were formally at least 144 operational aircrew on the base. In reality, there were considerably more in number; we had the various non-operational people in training, those declared fit for flying after a spell of illness or injury, and the 'odds and ends' left behind after the rest of their crews had completed their operational tours.

With those circumstances, I managed to put together a crew after a short period of bargaining. I then went to see Wacek, who would have a shrewd idea as to the chances of such a crew being accepted as a fully operational one. On this occasion he seemed satisfied.

'With this man as your temporary navigator, you should be all right,' he told me.

He was correct. Wlacek, let us call him, the son of a successful businessman, came to the squadron directly from a training unit. He had been recommended for an outstanding aptitude for navigational duties. He was tall, fair-haired, and very good-looking. He also spoke English fluently, having lived abroad before commencing his training in Britain.

But we had known one another previously, and I knew that he had a fear of flying which amounted to an obsession. I could understand and sympathise with this, and it did not prejudice me against him.

I did not tell Wacek that besides the navigator, I had been obliged to take on a pilot and subsequently an air gunner. The pilot, Josef, had completed an operational tour in Bomber Command. He then came to us for a second tour directly from the Blackpool depot. It had not seemed appropriate to send him to OTU, so now he eked out an occasional operational flight, and spent the rest of his time in the mess. Small, fine-boned, with a dark complexion, Josef was very sociable. He was always high in demand in the mess whenever a celebration was in the offing. He had become friendly enough with Wlacek to become part of the deal. The air gunner was a Pole from Brazil, popular for his general helpfulness and pleasant disposition. There was, however, considerable speculation about his age. To put it bluntly, he seemed ancient. It was said that his wrinkles were caused by the hot South American sun, not old age. As the maximum age for aircrew was thirty-two, we tried to think of him as just scraping in . . .

This ragged assortment somehow passed for a crew. Within three days we were down on the DROs, listed for an operation. The briefing was at midnight, the take-off at three a.m. I was intrigued – clearly, instead of a normal night patrol we would be flying most of the operation in daylight.

At the briefing, we found ourselves assigned to a 'Special Mission': a U-boat had been sighted close to Finisterre, the extreme north-western tip of Spain. Our job was to resume the search. I heard Wlacek murmuring quite audible obscenities at that point. I could understand why – he had not been on an operational flight before, and here we were, about to fly on search at the maximum range of the Mk XIV. At the best of times we were hardly keen on lingering close to the Spanish coast – a favourite hunting ground for Luftwaffe fighters.

Wlacek eyed me with suspicion, obviously thinking that I had deliberately asked him for this mission. But with Wlacek's excellent reputation for navigation, he would have been the ideal choice for the flight anyway.

Josef, who was to share the position of first pilot with me, showed no concern. He had come to the briefing straight from the mess, and would fly, as always, in his best blue – dress shoes, tie, and all the trappings. From his appearance, he might have been going to a dance in Barnstaple.

137

I was concerned. I recalled rumours of an occasion when he had mistaken a Royal Navy frigate for a U-boat. The subsequent attack apparently ended in a draw: he had bullet holes in his Wellington and the frigate suffered a dent. Luckily there were no casualties. A malicious impulse spurred me to mention it to him, but common sense prevailed.

I had previously agreed with Josef that I would pilot on the take-off while he would do so on landing. By the time the briefing had finished, I was less than happy about this arrangement: we were told that the strong, gusting cross-wind would increase further as the night set.

We ate our meal in morose silence. Even Wlacek had lost his eloquence. Only Josef appeared relaxed, and ate most of the food which the others left. Maybe he did think that he was going to a dance . . .

The weather was as promised. Gusts of strong wind kept me on the alert as I taxied to the take-off point. We began to roll at 3 a.m. sharp. At once I experienced the combined effect of starboard pull of the engines on full power and the cross-wind. With manipulation of the engine power and the rudder we just avoided being blown off the runway. Once the aircraft lifted off I gradually gained reasonable control over the heavy aircraft.

Wlacek, intent on saving petrol for the long flight ahead, insisted that we climb on higher than eight hundred feet. At that height the air turbulence was particularly trying, and I was not sorry to pass the controls over to Josef. He was instantly at home in the pilot's seat. He still cut an incongruous figure, dressed in his best jacket, and collar and tie. The only concession he made to being in an aircraft was wearing a flying helmet. I tried to look disapproving, but Josef was quite immune from such trivialities.

I went into the back of the aircraft, and was immediately collared by Wlacek.

'Look at this crappy flying'. he hissed into my ear, pointing to the gyro compass repeater on his bench. He turned the intercom on.

'Course 190° magnetic please, pilot', he said haughtily. Then to me, 'That is supposed to be our course. Do you think Josef knows that?'

I saw that Wrobel sat at the radar set. At least he could be counted on, I thought to myself. Another altercation broke out between Wlacek and Josef, and I made my way back to the cockpit. I realised that Josef remained essentially a bomber pilot. As yet he did not realise the importance of flying on an extremely accurate course for periods of many hours.

We bumped our way across the Bay. At the first sign of daylight we took up 'alert' positions. At 6.45 a.m., in full daylight, we were close to the Spanish coast. Here we entered a different phase of weather conditions – haze obscured the horizon, and even without clouds the visibility was poor.

Wlacek led us to the exact location of the U-boat sighting, then set the course for the first leg of the search. As the sun rose, the cockpit warmed up. Coastal turbulences intensified and spread out further into the sea. Soon we flew yet again amidst short, sharp and unpleasant bumps which never seemed to let up. The aircraft rode through the bumps uneasily, the wings flexing up and down. In the hot and hazy air we could but fly completely on instruments – altogether, not an enjoyable experience.

The unspoken tensions were all too evident. I counted on Wrobel's ability to see the fighters on the radar at a long distance. Meanwhile, we had one glimpse of the coast, blurred by the mist. On the sea, we could see nothing. At times there was no distinction between the sea and the air due to the haze.

'Fifteen more minutes', said Wlacek.

I was not sorry. We had been flying for over six hours, and we had a long way back home.

'Message from the Group: enemy aircraft in our patrol area', said the wireless operator.

'Oh, Jesus,' said Wlacek. 'How do you know that relates to us?'

'Because we're one of the aircraft listed by the Group', replied the wireless operator, sounding quite indignant.

'U-boat, three and a half miles, 90° port', Wrobel said suddenly.

'Attacking'. I said, pushing the throttles forward, and throwing the aircraft into a steep, diving turn.

'Where is she now?'

'Can't see, you're turning . . . yes, two miles, 10° port', Wrobel said, excitedly. 'Wait . . . the blip's already smaller, she's submerging.'

We were below one hundred feet, descending. With some surprise I noted that the sea was not still, but full of choppy, white waves.

'One mile, on course. She's gone.'

I had already closed the throttles and opened the bomb doors. The radio altimeter's red warning light was blinking. We were below fifty feet.

'Half a mile. Now', said Wrobel.

There were no signs on the sea's surface, at least not with our limited visibility. Wrobel could be a quarter of a mile out, easily. I shut the bomb door.

'Wireless operator, send a radar sighting message', I said. 'Wlacek, drop a flame float.'

'You're crazy,' he said. 'We've got enemy fighters around the corner.'

'You have to climb to at least 1,500 feet', the wireless operator said.

I looked at Josef, who raised his eyebrows and shrugged. He said nothing, and turned to searching the sky.

Ages seemed to pass. Wlacek had to estimate the position, then the wireless operator had to code it and send it off. At last the intercom came on.

'Message acknowledged by the Group. Their message continues: enemy fighters in your immediate vicinity. Fly 270°. Do not acknowledge.'

Once again, I began to dive into a turn.

'Turn to 220°', said Wlacek.

'Level her out', said Wrobel. 'I saw blips approx twenty miles, close to the coast.'

We waited in silence.

'Nothing', Wrobel reported.

I dived to fifty feet, lower, the throttles nearly full on. The aircraft vibrated wildly. After five minutes we changed the course to 270°. We had a long way back to fly now, the petrol would be rather short.

Twenty minutes later we were on a northerly course, heading for home, but still flying no higher than fifty feet. Josef took the controls. The weather began to improve, the air clearing and less bumpy. Thin cloud cover began to appear on the horizon. Josef increased the height to between one hundred and two hundred feet. Wlacek instantly came to life, and spent as much time as possible correcting Josef's course.

Hours passed and the bickering continued before Wrobel reported the Scilly Isles ahead. By now we were into the tenth hour of the flight.

Josef landed the aircraft smoothly and confidently. I had a momentary feeling that his mastery of the aircraft might have been well in advance of mine. On our way to the debriefing, Wlacek looked grim and not too friendly. We learned that two more crews were being diverted to continue the search for the U-boat.

The crew I had put together made no further flights. I carried on looking for alternative arrangements. Wlacek applied for a posting to a long range navigational unit, and was somewhat shocked to find himself accepted. Josef resumed his enjoyable and civilised way of life both in and out of operations, and when the air gunner finished his tour there were stories of him retiring to a rest home . . .

*

Not unnaturally the war did not stand still while we were pre-occupied with our tiny fraction of it. In Italy the Allied forces were bled heavily while fighting their way up north. A Polish division became involved in a particularly vicious confrontation with the Germans at Monte Cassino. By the time the Poles won through they had left a large part of the division on the slopes of the mountain. They subsequently felt that they deserved a clear recognition of their contribution, but it was so diluted when it came that they were angry and confused. The edges seemed fudged, the main issue obscured. World politics would see to it that less and less account was taken of the contributions of the likes of the Poles in the war effort.

At that point most of us realised that the demonic energy of the Germans was dwindling. From now on, in spite of any blunders, the West with its material and technological advantage, and the Russians by sheer numbers and determination would apply a tighter and tighter grip on the Germans. What would happen to Poland? Very few people I knew wanted to speculate about the future. It was difficult enough to keep up with the present. Even at our station a great deal was happening about which I knew little. We had hardly any idea how the Canadians and English squadrons stationed with us were coping. Occasionally we heard of their losses or their attacks on U-boats.

We had in common inexplicable losses of aircraft which disappeared without a trace. Flying at 500 feet during the night in all weathers was probably enough to account for most of the aircraft, and enemy action the others. But somehow, after working one's way through the technicalities such generalisations did not seem adequate. While looking through air intelligence monthly reports I came across statistics on air/sea rescue operations. After the type by type breakdown of the aircraft involved one element was all too clear. There were no rescues from the Wellington Mk XIV at all. Coincidence? I checked through more data. In total I found only two cases where the crews were saved. The small print told me that both these rescues were carried out in shallow water fairly near the coast. What had happened to the others?

My guesses focused on the recent modifications made on the Mk XIV: the front turret had been replaced by a perspex nose, a retractable turret was built into the fuselage for the Leigh Light. In ditching the nose would break under the pressure of the water, while the severe stress of hitting the sea would almost certainly break the fuselage in two. The nose, with the heavy engines, would go down at once, taking the dinghy with it; the tail section could not float by itself.

At the time, no one was particularly concerned with this problem. If the propellers did not kill the pilots in a crash, the depth
charges we carried might. Then there was the petrol tank in the
bomb bay . . . And if we were flying at 500 feet we had a maximum of fifteen seconds until we hit the sea, on a good day. In
trouble there would be but a sudden splash . . .

On my next leave I was off to Grantham where Geniek was completing his SFTS on Miles Masters. He was doing very well; he
had great potential, his aggressive nature being matched by self-
control. I was pleased for him, and we consumed a great deal of
alcohol and shot unending lines.

I returned to the squadron to find that there was still no permanent navigator available for us. Again we went onto the 'hire
out' scheme, where each one of us flew with anyone, anywhere,
anytime. Apart from training flights we flew such operational
flights as were available to us. Thus I flew as a first pilot with a
crew whose captain had just returned from some course or
other. It was a time when a change in tactics brought us to 'box
patrol' flying; these were rectangular flight paths which could
take one or more hours to complete. One then went around and
around again depending on the size of the rectangle and its distance from the base.

A large number of such boxes covered the whole of the Bay of
Biscay area operating twenty-four hours a day thus saturating the
western approaches to France with anti-submarine patrols. This
was certainly bad news for the U-boats, but it came at a time
when things were not so good for us either. A complication arose
which ensured that no one would be bored or inattentive at
his job.

It concerned a plague of engine trouble, a black death according to the alarmists. Briefly it related to the fact that during the
war it was rarely possible to put together all the advances in
technology at the same time in one area of need. In our case the
more powerful engines on the Mk XIV needed a better and more
efficient grade of petrol for Coastal Command's conditions of

long-term, economical speed flying. Otherwise, as large amounts of lower grade fuel were consumed by the engines the carbon deposited on the spark plugs created serious problems. What was immediately needed was a suitable additive for the petrol we were using. That was to be in the future. We soon began to think that we would not be seeing much of it anyway. The reality of the present was rather harsh.

CHAPTER TEN

Routine Patrols

One day I was off on the new 'box patrol'. I had of course heard of the engine problems and forced landings, but I was only too pleased to go on an operation, and could but hope that I would not become involved in any mishaps.

We took off in the evening. I flew the aircraft to the patrol area, then changed over with the second pilot. We had barely done this when the aircraft trembled slightly, just as I was reaching for the inevitable cup of coffee. I froze. The engines worked smoothly, and all seemed well. Minutes passed. Another tremor. I stood up and examined the instruments. Nothing. Another ten minutes. Then suddenly, quietly, the port engine died on us.

The aircraft swung around while we pilots scrambled frantically. I had no time to connect the intercom, too busy manipulating the throttles. Four hundred feet, speed now falling, the engines refusing to respond. Worse, the controls would not budge. Sweat poured down into my eyes. What was wrong? Any moment we would reach the stalling speed. At night, at this height, we would hit the sea before the crew had time to realise what was happening. The great, the one and only splash. At that moment I realised what was wrong with the controls; the second pilot, unknown to me, had switched to the automatic pilot, something I never did at night. I groped around in the dark cockpit, desperately trying to find the right switch. At last.

The engine continued to spit and backfire. I let the aircraft swing around to face the land. Only 200 miles to go. We were now 300 feet above the sea, instruments haywire due to the fact that the now defunct port engine powered a range of electrical

145

equipment. I jettisoned the bombs. This cost me another seventy-five feet, but if I was hoping to ditch if all else failed it was not the best idea to do it with six armed depth charges on board. I gunned the engine. It was not happy, but who cared as long as there was some power to be extracted from it?

I plugged the intercom in to discover that a message had already gone out to the Group, and a course to the nearest aerodrome was given to me. I continued to gun the sick engine. This alone was an alarming activity at night, watching the sparks and flames belching out of the glowing exhaust, the engine trembling. We gradually managed to climb to 1,000 feet, which seemed a luxury. As we were now transmitting at regular intervals to allow the Group to monitor our position it also meant that we were likely to be followed by the Germans, and their reaction to our plight was an entirely different matter. But our luck held out, and the engine picked up, allowing us to reach the base after some nine hours of flying.

After that flight I began to take a great interest in the squadron operations in relation to the engine problems. The extent of the problems was rather alarming. Hardly a day passed without at least one crew running into trouble. One day a crew did not return. No one knew why. The same day I was off on another operation with the crew from the previous flight.

The weather forecast was very nasty. I had a bad feeling over this flight and could hardly eat my meal. I felt very much alone. By now the second pilot was worried to the point where he could freeze or do something irreversibly wrong in the air. We had no time to correct mistakes. Certainly there was no room for histrionics in our type of flying. The crew seemed especially anxious also, chain-smoking, leaving their food.

We flew directly west after take-off in late evening. Within an hour, as the darkness fell, we entered into a warm weather system. With the depression deepening the disturbances grew rapidly in strength until I considered it no longer safe to stay at 500 feet. As we increased our height the violence of the storm grew also. One could lose 500 feet in a single turbulence. The crew was silent. They disapproved of my continuing the patrol in such a storm, and who could blame them? How long could the aircraft stand up to the viciousness of the turbulence? We seemed to be testing the aircraft to its limits. I knew this. I also knew that we could not turn back.

At the moment when we were being lifted by the air current the port engine chose to fail, without a bang but with a whimper. It kicked, milled, roared up and worked intermittently. We managed to reach 2,000 feet, but while doing so the starboard engine failed also. For a time we seemed to be thrown around the sky by the rough air, the engines milling uselessly.

This time there was no panic. There would be no ditching on a night like this. I lowered the flaps slightly and continued to manipulate the throttles; surely at least one engine would pick up, then with jettisoning everything . . . Yet I must have thought us doomed, for I was slightly irritated by the wireless operator when he sent an SOS message. I could see no point in making a fuss.

Nevertheless we jettisoned the depth charges. The engines stuttered and threw out flames, then came back to life. We made our way to the base landing, arriving at 04.00. Eight hours of flying.

I hardly believed I was there. When the engines finally cut, silence fell on us at the dispersal point. The ground crews shook their heads and averted their eyes. There was nothing anyone could have done for us.

Training again, this time a longish spell of low level bombing. The exercises needed no navigator, and were primarily meant for the pilots to acquire sufficient skill in dropping bombs on very small targets at low altitudes. Those of the crew who did have to come with me did not care for the experience. I was hardly surprised. The target was located in a tiny cove surrounded by cliffs. The approach was from the open sea, at only a few feet above the sea itself, the height at which all the course correction had to be done. Having dropped the bomb one then had to make a very steep climb, turning on full power, dive seawards and repeat the process. While I returned tired out, the crew were green-faced.

147

We found a navigator for a shortish and uneventful operation over the Bay, and then it was back for another operation with the 'twin engine failure' crew. I went to the briefing in trepidation; the crew were jinxed, no doubt about that. What would it be this time? Could things get worse?

One glance at the route told me that they could indeed get worse. We were being sent on a one-off mission: that of tracking the German radar. Our briefing was simple enough: get to the French coast on the Channel along by Brittany, then fly along the coast eastwards for some sixty miles, turn back and repeat the flight as many times as possible in seven hours' flying time. An additional aerial on the aircraft and a special device installed above the navigator's table would do the rest.

We hardly looked at each other during the briefing. Another crew had tried to do a similar trip not long ago. Even though they had returned, their plane was so shot up that it was unbelievable how they did.

The night was clear, the air still. Off we went over the coast, then down to fifty feet towards France. There could be no tricks or dodging for us; our coastal radar would be tracking us. I took the plane up to 500 feet. I could see the French coast clearly. Almost at once a red light came on on the device, a signal that the German radar had begun to track us. The radar operator continued to report blips and signals which we noted but could not investigate.

After nearly two hours and something like five runs up and down the coast I saw a flash of a small yellow light on the coast, as did the other members of the crew. Then another yellow light flashed on, this time exactly at the turning point. Were we being signalled, or being tracked? The crew speculated rather nervously, but we stayed on course and at the same height. But not for long. The Germans had had enough of us at last. We had of course been briefed on the various German coastal defences; as always they were extremely efficient in improved extensions of conventional weapons. One example was the 'silber ferries', floating platforms packed with low level rapid-fire cannons and machine guns. Whatever it was now, they let us have the lot;

tracers of all sorts and colours curving towards us from various places all at the same time. We dived, turned, and twisted away at full throttle, came back, and were pasted again. In my mind I was composing a dramatic message to the Group, but before I could get around to sending it the Group lost nerve on our behalf and recalled us. I could not move away from the coast fast enough.

*

At Chivenor, we were aware of being part of the most advanced anti U-boat centre of Coastal Command. No fewer than three squadrons were continuously stationed there, all fitted with the latest anti-submarine equipment and instrumentation. The first attacks by Leigh Light equipped and radar-guided aircraft were carried out by Wellingtons stationed in Chivenor as early as 1942.

Despite the considerable number of attacks on U-boats by the Chivenor-based squadrons, I could not help noticing, when reading the monthly intelligence reports, that the Liberators were more successful than Wellingtons. This was understandable – the Liberators patrolled the mid-Atlantic area of merchant shipping convoys, where the U-boats were forever present.

At times I was rather envious of the Liberator pilots. They had a large, four-engined aircraft, more comfortable than the Wellington, with controls which were much more easy to handle than ours. If the Wellington was the equivalent of the Royal Navy's frigates, then the Liberators were the cruisers.

But no matter which aircraft one flew in, the attacks on U-boats rarely had any common denominator. Even sightings of submarines could not be said to conform to any particular stereotype. Examples of the differences in attacks, battles and sightings abounded even in our squadron.

Flight Officer Leszek Miedzybrodsky joined the squadron in Predannack. By the time I got back from OTU, he and his crew were well into their operational tour. I soon came to know Leszek, mainly through two of his crew. They were young, cheerful extroverts, and I grew particularly friendly with Zyg Frylinski, Leszek's wireless operator. Marginally impressed by my status, Zyg introduced me to his first pilot.

Leszek kept a low profile on the whole, but proved to be friendly, with a direct approach to people and a dry wit. In civilian life he had been an engineering consultant, specialising in aircraft engine design. By our standards he was ancient, and as he was rather bald we surmised that he did not have long to go. For his part, Leszek showed considerable forbearance with the younger aircrew, and his room became a popular meeting place for a cup of good coffee and the latest squadron gossip. Often Leszek would observe our youthful antics with a look of mild amusement, and I was much impressed by his tolerance.

On 28th April 1944, Leszek and his crew took off for the routine anti-submarine sweep over the Bay of Biscay. At the time I was still without a permanent navigator, so I filled in on a variety of tasks. That day I was sent to Silloth to ferry pilots back and forth as well as spares needed by the OTU.

When I returned the following day, Zyg was waiting for me, hopping about in a frenzy of excitement; they had sighted and attacked a U-boat. He had been at the radar at the time – he had seen the blip, then directed the pilot towards the submarine.

'Top this one then, Mr Pilot', he cried triumphantly. 'You may be a captain, but where were you when all the action was going on?' He danced around me in ecstasy.

When Zyg had calmed down, he described the attack in more detail. It had been a very good attack by any standards. Quiet air and a still sea surface contributed to a good radar picture. Zyg had seen the blip at twenty miles, almost at the limits of the radar's resolving power, which gave them plenty of time to go through the correct drill.

'But then the U-boat spotted us . . . at the last stage of the approach', Zyg said, grinning. 'The blip began to disappear. I thought I'd lost it. Then the second pilot saw the wake of the sub. The conning tower had already gone.'

They had dived to fifty feet and attacked, dropping all six depth charges.

'We turned on the Leigh Light and searched the surface, but we couldn't see anything. We rechecked the area – no trace of it.'

Somewhat disappointed but not entirely displeased, they had turned for home finally. Even with no damage ascertained, they had still served the purpose of keeping the submarine under the surface.

'Well, that's your lot for this tour', I said, spitefully.

Zyg shook his head, then laughed. 'You're just jealous . . . You'll never even see a sub at the rate you're going.'

Officially, 304 Squadron had an encounter with a U-boat once in every forty operational flights, or one per 350 operational flying hours. These figures bear out the feeling we had that even a sighting was a rare occurrence.

Two weeks passed. During that period I became accident prone, experiencing single and double engine failure, as well as narrowly escaping an enemy fighter. I felt drained of energy and was quite pessimistic about my chances of survival. Even Zyg noticed my state of mind, and stopped teasing me. When I was posted for another flight we both strained to look cheerful about my prospects.

In contrast, Leszek and his crew had flown several uneventful operations. The day before I was due to fly again, they had another flight. They took off at 9 p.m. Night and late evening take-offs were greatly helped by the Drem System – Chivenor's night flying lights – one of the best systems in use at the time. The long runway facing the sea also proved useful, giving the heavy aircraft plenty of time to raise its speed.

Most pilots were happy to have any additional aid in getting the Mk XIV off the ground. With its extra equipment – depth charges, Leigh Light turret, the complex radar gear and radar 'chain' in the nose, as well as additional petrol tank and machine guns and ammunition – the aircraft was definitely not at its best during the take-off.

The next morning Zyg woke me up with breakfast. He looked

pale and tired, and his usual high spirits were nowhere in evidence. As soon as I was fully awake and had drunk my coffee, he dragged me out towards the Flying Control Tower, where their badly damaged aircraft stood; the fabric torn in many places. My eyes widened as I inspected it. Zyg shook his head as though he could hardly believe what had taken place. I waited for him to start talking.

Within an hour of their take-off they had arrived at their patrol area, which they circled until 3 a.m.

'Then we spotted a blip, five miles away, 90° to starboard. The next minute there was another, five and a half miles away. It was quite light – there was a full moon, and the sea was calm.'

The crew had searched the sea seeing nothing at first. Some broken cloud cover created pockets of deep shadow on the surface.

'Leszek took the aircraft down towards the first blip, while we went through the attack drill. Leszek saw them both, almost at the same time. Two U-boats', Zyg exclaimed. 'Can you believe it? Both on the surface, as well. It seemed like such good luck. . .'

They had the idea that they would sink one, and bring in other aircraft and the navy for the other. It was going to be the Big Event.

'But the bloody Jerries didn't fancy being blown up. They were only a couple of hundred yards apart, and they both opened up on us with everything they had.'

Multicoloured tracers poured in towards them. The aircraft shook.

'Direct hits, so many we lost count. Sparks from electrical equipment were flying everywhere, fumes began to fill the plane. We were rushing about with fire extinguishers, but no one panicked and everyone did his job.'

Leszek retained control over the bucking aircraft with difficulty. There was severe structural damage, and some of the controls had ceased to function. Depth charges straddled one U-boat.

'The rear gunner had a fire fight going with the subs, the explosions from the depth charges – it was quite a spectacle.'

At fifty feet, in the dark, with a damaged aircraft, things looked grim. Leszek turned the plane around towards England. The engines seemed to function well enough, but there was a long journey home ahead of them.

'I never thought that we'd make it back . . . I was sure we'd have to ditch her. The plane shook all the way back, but we gained height, and then just hoped for the best.'

The national press covered the story. Zyg bounded up to me with a paper.

'Look, I'm famous', he cackled.

'You seem to have recovered', I said.

'Oh, it's just routine for me, you know. Next time the Jerries won't get off so lightly . . .'

I am not aware of Leszek receiving any decorations or promotion following the attack, but he continued to prove his excellent flying standards, and eventually became a test pilot for the RAF at Boscombe Down.

One of the most successful attacks by 304 Squadron took place soon after Leszek's – on 18th June 1944, twelve days after D-Day. Since June 6th, our anti-submarine patrols had been stepped up considerably. On the same night as this attack took place, I was on a patrol assigned to the Channel area, where Coastal Command aimed to block the access of U-boats to the armada of ships carrying men and equipment to France.

The aircraft piloted by Flight Lieutenant Leopold Antoniewicz left the aerodrome at 9.10 p.m. Within one hour their radar had failed, but good night visibility led the crew to decide to continue with the patrol. The subsequent sighting and attack were thus carried out without the benefit of the complex and expensive gadgetry installed in the Mk XIV aircraft.

According to the pilot's report, visibility was four to five miles at the time, with clouds at two thousand feet. The pilot was the first to sight the U-boat, which was coming to the surface at three miles. He dived to attack it. While still one mile from the target, both the second pilot and the navigator observed another submarine surfacing at approximately one and a half miles. The pilot continued with the attack on the first submarine. The depth charges were dropped, and from the reports of the crew practically blew the U-boat into pieces.

The attack was subsequently confirmed by the Admiralty. The total time for the attack, from the moment of the sighting until the explosions had finished, was a mere three minutes.

CHAPTER ELEVEN

Facets of War

Shortly before D-Day there was a change in squadron comman-
ders. Korbut left for a high office in the Air Ministry. The new CO
was a bird of totally different feathers. He was much more
devoted to ensuring that the wheels of the organisation ran
smoothly, and that the right people saw who was turning them.
Not surprisingly he was less keen on the young volunteers. At the
first parade he addressed us along the following lines:

'As of now, I want to see the aircrew show more discipline. In
future, officers will stand on the right in parades, and NCOs on
the left. And I expect the aircrew to wear the eagles and badges of
their Polish ranks on their battledress from here on. After all, we
have our own Air Force here. There are to be no RAF insignia
worn on any occasion.'

An incident some days later further illustrated his different
attitude towards aircrew and operational flying. We were due to
take off from the shortest runway facing the hills at the Chivenor
aerodrome. The air was completely still, and without the wind in
front of us and the added weight of the overloaded aircraft, the
take-off would be more difficult than usual.

The aircraft had only just begun to move forward when there
was a loud bang from behind us. I shut the throttles and we
rolled to a stop. A quick discussion with the crew followed. We
could find no apparent fault. Nevertheless, at that point I could
have scrapped the operation and returned to the hangar for a full
inspection of the aircraft. However, not having broken the radio
silence, I decided that we would go on with the operation. We returned to the take-off point, and this time the take-off went
smoothly.

Having cleared the hill-tops we set our course. Next morning, after eleven hours of uneventful flying we landed safely back at the base. No sooner had we touched down when I was called to the office of the Wing Commander. To my astonishment he gave a short speech:

'I watched your antics last night. In future I'm not having any pilot returning for a second take-off. I'm giving you an order that from now on you must take off immediately . . . Understand?'

We turned to various friends for help in finding ourselves a navigator. Then things began to happen that were mostly outside my sphere of control. Our navigator arrived at last, a hard-working engineer, in his last year of degree study when the war broke out. We had two weeks to train him. Meanwhile the operations continued at full strength. The squadron attacked two U-boats, and Ochalski was yet again attacked by a Ju88 which pressed the attack very hard, but he returned safely.

With the invasion of the Continent approaching, the American Army, who until now had filled every available space in the vicinity, was packing and leaving for the invasion harbours. In many ways I was sorry to see them go. I had become friendly with some American officers, and at one stage was allowed by the CO to take them up on training flights.

Only then did I realise what an experience flying in a warplane was to many people. I could hardly keep my face straight while listening to their excited voices on the intercom. I let them fire the guns from the rear turret, and took them for the inevitable low pass over their camp. This they enjoyed hugely, observing with great glee the commotion we caused. From then on I had a supply of free cigarettes, and was regularly taken for free drinks to Barnstaple, where I postured in expensive places.

The operational pace of the squadron intensified. We were at our wits' end without the navigator. We wanted to bring him in, but he was not to be rushed.

The aerodrome was packed with aircraft, and everyone was suffering from pre-invasion fever. All aircraft were on immediate standby, and stood around in large groups, fully bombed up and refuelled.

Under such overcrowded conditions the not unexpected disaster finally struck: On a clear day, as we were having our Sunday lunch, we heard a loud engine roar followed by grating noises. A Mk XIV from an English squadron had burst a tyre on landing and ploughed into a group of bombed-up aircraft.

We rushed out in time to see explosions, fires, chaos. Ambulances, fire brigades and more explosions followed. Pieces of aircraft flew through the air. Black smoke covered the countryside. Of the crew no trace was found. Three fully loaded aircraft disappeared in the holocaust.

That evening we went on a Channel patrol. A heavy sea mist sat over the whole of the patrol area. At around 04.00 hours Nikel decided to go into the back of the aircraft. He had hardly moved away when the darkness was disturbed by a sudden explosion. Nikel was at my side in a moment. Strong smell of petrol. Port engine boost control fell to zero. I scanned the instruments, listened to the engines; all seemed all right. We had to open the cockpit windows to try to clear the smell of petrol, but to no avail. Where was the petrol escaping from?

Fumes poured non-stop into the aircraft. Puzzled, worried yet embarrassed, we returned to base. It was an uneasy flight, the fumes persisting, the wind howling through the cockpit. I made a cautious approach, but of course could not stop sparks and flames from the exhausts. We touched down after an eternal seven and a half hours.

In a follow up inquiry we found out what had happened. Nikel, while walking past the wireless operator where the corridor was at its narrowest, brushed against the side of the aircraft where the exposed pipes and electrical wires met. By a one in a million chance a wire broke, sparked, and melted a tube leading petrol vapour to the petrol gauge. Why the fumes, together with us, had not ignited was a mystery. Following this incident the squadron engineers placed covers on most of the exposed electrical wiring in these aircraft.

We then flew two more operations in quick succession, each with a different navigator, each over ten hours in duration. Then our navigator joined us and we did a few days and nights of five hour training flights. Then we were operational and off to the Bay of Biscay, this time with a difference – in the daytime.

It turned out to be a busy day, the crew dutifully following each blip, the gunners gyrating their turrets non-stop. The eleven hour flight was exhausting, and the next followed the same pattern as well as length.

The more experienced crews were kept even more busy. One homed in on two U-boats, saw them in full moonlight and attacked without resorting to the use of the Leigh Light. Another crew had its attack confirmed by the Admiralty as having sunk a U-boat, a feat of considerable magnitude.

Kieltyka and his crew went from strength to strength. Yet again they attacked a U-boat. We were therefore mystified to hear that they had not returned from an operation. What could have happened to them? They had baled out over Eire. They were indestructible.

Three days later they were back in the squadron and starting out on operations again. All except for the second pilot, who had injured his back on landing. In spite of various treatments he was eventually grounded permanently.

We then began flights deep into the Atlantic. Although the plague of engine trouble was contained, it was not completely overcome. It could certainly not be forgotten. The immediate threat from enemy fighters lessened, but flying 500 or 600 miles into the Atlantic at 500 feet was not exactly a relaxing way of spending the night, especially in gales or very low cloud cover.

These patrols were alternated with Channel patrols. Those concerned the protection of the massive fleets of the Royal Navy, close to the French coast at night, bombarding the German positions deep inland. Each time we went we were regaled by the sight of the warships returning to the English coast in the early morning light. Stretching in a line, reaching as far as one could see, it was certainly a stirring and unforgettable sight, no matter where one's home was.

*

At last D-Day came. Frenetic activity in our white planes with black bands painted on for the occasion. The armada of warships continued to bombard the Germans long after the invasion had started. The activity continued when I returned to the Channel a few days after the invasion. Chivenor was busy, non-stop, day and night. At that stage I cannot remember any operations being washed out due to the weather. We were simply told what the conditions were like in the patrol area, and off we went.

I was due for another leave. I left for London as the first step in keeping an appointment; I was to go to see Aniela and a friend and have dinner with them. I had already learned of the 'arrangement' which Aniela had with a Pilot Officer called Leszek Suchy, newly stationed at a squadron near London. I looked forward to the dinner, but had some reservations about it. One did not have to be too perceptive to see that Aniela had made her decisions and set the path of her life accordingly. I was not too keen to be preached at, even by a good-looking girl. But there seemed to be nothing really unusual about the invitation.

The door had hardly opened when I was embraced by Aniela, an experience which instantly unnerved me. She was a young desirable woman, and I was still somewhere amongst the crews of airmen committed to the invasion of the Continent. I was rather bowled over. Leszek turned out to be a tall, ascetic-looking young man with a calm manner.

I could not understand this. I examined Aniela as if I had not met her before. She could surely not be the person whom I had known before. What had made her do it? This posturing young officer with the handsome profile was just too much. An architect, so what did that mean these days? One stray bullet, one pilot's misjudgement and good-bye for ever. At first I was speechless with anger, frustration and disappointment. I sat there, gulping down the drinks silently.

It turned out that the dinner was a deliberate affair to celebrate my Imieniny (Saint's Day). Even Leszek permitted himself the thinnest of smiles at seeing me so flustered. Unfortunately I made the inevitable error.

'How did you remember after all these years?' I stuttered.

159

Aniela flashed me a smile.

'How did you forget in such a short spell of time?' she said, and sat down next to me. We drank wodka. Leszek disappeared into the kitchen.

Aniela lit a cigarette in the style of the time. She sat very close to me, her leg touching mine. I heard Leszek busy in their little kitchen. Roast chicken, straight from the farm, negotiated at a very high price.

'Josek,' she said, pressing her leg a little harder against mine, 'congratulations.'

'On what?' I asked cautiously.

'You've achieved what most young men want these days: you're a pilot, captain of a crew, you're well into your operational flying, and you're not even twenty-one. Leszek,' she called out, and put her arm around my neck.

'Yes, darling?'

'Josek is really something; so devoted, and still a sergeant to prove it.' No answer from the kitchen.

Aniela had hugged me before . . . she was fourteen years old at the time.

'Well . . .' She tightened her grip on my neck, not an unpleasant experience. 'Give me a kiss, the way you used to.'

'I never . . .'

'Leszek,' she called, 'Josek refuses to kiss me. He used to hug me ever so close.' I heard Leszek open the door. Aniela held me tight. I felt myself blush.

'Aniela,' I said, 'let go of me.'

'You're disgusting,' she said. 'Next thing you'll be wanting to make love to me. Just because it's your Imieniny. You men are . . .'

At a loss for words, I turned to Leszek.

'If you go on like this,' he said, 'Geniek will run away. We'll have to eat the chicken by ourselves.' She let go.

The meal, cooked in Polish style, was excellent, with the various peculiarities which mark cooking from one particular corner of the world. But I could no longer relax, especially as a woman's presence becomes even more prominent under the cir-

160

. firing a Bren gun at
U.

. at decoration parade
U receiving the Cross of
ur.

rior of a troop-carrying
wick.

Our navigator, T. Streng. pilot's cockpit can be see the background.

A Warwick at Chedburgh (Transport Command).

Warwick GR

cumstances of a meal. I sensed Aniela's sharp thoughts ready to strike. It was like being over the Bay at sunrise.

Leszek was so polished and civilised that I could read no signals from him except straightforward hospitality. But then, he would be a lot more at ease here than in the squadron.

'All right, Aniela,' he said. 'Now sit down on Geniek's knee and get the knife out.'

'As if I cared,' she said.

She did sit down on my knees, then ran her fingers around my RAF pilot's badge. Leszek poured us all liqueurs and sighed.

'Aniela . . .' he said. Aniela began to speak clearly, soberly.

'Honestly, Josek,' she began, 'it hurts me to see you so muddled.' She felt heavy on my knees. I shifted.

'Sit still,' she said, rather softly. 'For God's sake, show a little understanding. There is a real world, back in Poland. This . . .' she fingered my badge, 'is dreamland.'

'Some of us die in this dreamland.'

She lifted herself to pick up a cigarette.

'Why don't you take off your jacket and make yourself comfortable?' said Leszek amiably. 'Aniela is only winding herself up.' I could not raise a smile.

'Do you know how I came to be here in England?' she asked me. 'I'm one of the couriers who bring evidence – photographs, and so on – into the West from Poland. A lot of people risk their lives to get the likes of me here. Back there they live on hopes, the first one being that the Poles in the West will let the public know what's happening over there.'

'Well. . .?'

'Well, what? Firstly, the English took weeks to debrief me. Do you know how many Poles are hanged, shot and tortured in that space of time? When I finally made my way to our people who should have helped, they turned out to be useless; proud, unbending, in their ancient uniforms, their command of English worse than mine. Their understanding of the West is absolutely pathetic. They're caught and ground up by events far beyond their comprehension.

'I did talk to the English and American journalists; cautious,

161

blasé vultures. They would not touch such material with a barge pole, they said. Atrocity stories are just not on – First World War stuff, you know, darling; it used to be all that stuff about the German soldiers bayoneting children and raping nuns. What finally broke me up was the village destroyed by the SS as a reprisal – this in a country with a long record of co-operation with the Germans.

'Just about then I saw you in London, and then I realised how completely alone we really are. Nobody would do anything for us. The West does not listen to people like me. They are so terribly self-centred; they will buy an expensive bouquet to put on our grave, in the cemetery of our country.' She stopped. She had calmed down now.

Now Leszek picked up the theme. 'We looked to the West for culture, the philosophy of life, civilisation. You should know it; Aniela tells me you knew French very early in your life. Our people still put their faith in the West . . .'

'I don't know,' said Aniela. 'Even we began to realise that it is no good screaming in French when the Gestapo is breaking your bones. I've seen enough here to understand that there may be power and riches here, but none of the sympathy that drives you to help those in need. Without that, no one is going to stick their neck out to save us.'

All at once she turned on me again. 'You will not have to queue with a coffin, waiting to be hanged,' she said. 'Back in our country, patriots die slowly, in agony, alone. What do you think sustains them?'

Leszek, who had been filling glasses with hot *krupnik*, chose that moment to pass them around. By then I had recovered somewhat.

'Perhaps you're the dreamer,' I said. 'What are you trying to do? Make me feel personally responsible for the agonies of our nation?'

'Just to be aware of them', Aniela said, softly. 'And act when the time is right.' I dared not ask what she meant. A silence followed. Aniela sat between me and Leszek. For a moment I felt

162

as if I were in harmony with them, as though I understood them.

*

Two days before going on my next leave we flew deep into the Atlantic, and had to cross a storm on the way. This had to be the worst storm ever, or so it felt at the time. A monstrous cumulonimbus sat straight on our track. Previous experience told me that we would not be able to fly around it without totally disrupting the whole flight schedule. But no previous experience helped us in facing the fury of the winds, air currents and countercurrents. Hail hammered against the fabric of the aircraft. Flashes of lightning were ceaseless. We flew directly into the storm.

As we flew I struggled to keep the aircraft flying. I had no particular thought as to what might lie ahead. Everything in the aircraft needed instant attention. Soon I was wet with perspiration and with the water coming into the cockpit. After a while I noticed sparks and flashes of light darting along the cockpit window. Gradually the propellers began to glow, the intensity of the light increasing rapidly. Finally the aircraft was cocooned in a glowing, eerie bluish light. I felt tremendously uneasy, not knowing what we should do. Meanwhile, the intensity of the light reached a brilliant peak. There was a very loud noise. A stream of light entered the cockpit and disappeared down the corridor, into the fuselage. Complete darkness followed.

'Christ,' said the navigator. 'The damn thing passed right by my chair.'

'Examine the aircraft for damage,' I said.

'What's happened?' asked the wireless operator. 'I was nearly blown out of the aircraft.'

'We were struck by lightning', I replied.

'Well, couldn't you have told me?' he said, plaintively.

The wireless operator found that his aerial was burnt out. No other damage was found. The radar operator had prudently switched off his set as soon as he realised that the electrical

163

disturbances were unusually high.

We broke out of the storm in time to meet an unreal sight, that of a fully lighted Red Cross ship. But as soon as the radar operator reported another aircraft in the vicinity we turned back to the patrol.

At last we turned around to head back to base. I gave the controls to Nikel and prepared to relax with a cup of coffee and a cigarette. But not for long. An argument developed between Nikel and the navigator. Like all of us, Nikel was tired by then, and did not really want to be at the controls. Now he flew badly, and the infuriated navigator became abusive. Dutifully, I took the controls over again. Something told me that in the daylight I would have seen Nikel wink and grin.

After my leave I was picked up at Barnstaple station by the squadron transport. The driver, Mr Matiszek, knew me rather well. We sat in silence for such a long time that I perceived something was wrong.

'Cigarette, Mr Matiszek?'

'Thank you, Mr Jaworski', he said. 'Well, you might as well hear it from me as anyone else; we lost two crews last week.'

'Run of bad luck, Mr Matiszek.'

'Well, yes, just what one of the crews . . . Mr Wacek . . .'

'Wacek?' I sat up. 'Wacek? No, you can't kill Wacek.' He said nothing. 'Who else?'

'Bronek.' We sat in silence for the rest of the journey. It was a glorious summer day. As we reached the aerodrome Wellingtons were flying around, the sound of their engines reverberated through the valley.

The crew was back. Nikel was married, and talked of bringing his wife to Barnstaple. People seemed to studiously avoid the topic of the missing crews. At that I went to see a senior pilot I had known well since joining the squadron. He gave me a large glass of cognac.

'They're all dead, you know,' he said, brutally. 'We searched the area at least twice.'

'And Bronek?'

He shrugged. 'They just disappeared. Not a signal, nothing.'

We then flew seven consecutive operational flights, with no more than one day off between each. Fatigue brought on a sense of unreality. The squadron, now at its peak of performance, flew patrols covering twenty-four hours every day. Some of the Channel patrols still had a good deal of excitement in them. The Channel Islands continued to be occupied by the Germans, who did not exactly approve of such patrols. Their flak was intense and accurate, and adapted to cover all heights from deck level up.

A night on a close to shore patrol was thus far from boring. At 500 feet there was a great deal that AA could attempt to do. I found on one such patrol that 'corkscrewing' over a five hour period was very tiring, and the anticipation of the next pasting quite unnerving. However, we went on the Channel operations four times. By then we were a senior crew in the squadron, and as such were high on the list for these flights.

On 1st August 1944, the news of the Warsaw uprising had reached us. The prolonged agony of the people in that city where nearly 300,000 men, women and children were murdered while the whole world watched created a range of reactions amongst the Poles in Britain.

For some time I had had no communication from Aniela. One evening I phoned the White Eagle club. No, they had not seen her for some time. They could not recall for how long, nor did they know where she might be now. I made no further enquiries.

During late August Nikel left us for the OTU. He was not sorry to go, and said so. His wife was now expecting, and a three month break was very timely.

On our first operation with our new second pilot we came back in very bad weather, the decision on whether to land at base being left to the pilot's discretion. With visibility near zero at ground level, I was led into the estuary by the radar operator. Flying on instruments below the level of the hills on the first approach, I had but a glimmer of the emergency aerodrome lights turned on for my benefit. After three attempts I caught up with the boundary lights, and stayed with them at 150 feet, made

165

the full landing drill and landed from that height. All this virtuoso performance was lost on the second pilot, who could hardly stifle his yawns at the end of such a boring flight.

However, he came to life on the next flight when we had engine trouble after some two hours into the Atlantic. Daylight made the scene starker, the problem easier to handle. The engine refused to pick up, and what with the rather clumsy change-over we were down to 150 feet, five seconds from the sea at the most before I managed to stabilise the aircraft.

Sweat poured down my face so hard that I could taste it. My right leg was visibly trembling. We had jettisoned the depth charges, and were trying to lose as much fuel as possible. We had sent an SOS message, including our position, in plain language. I had given the order to prepare for ditching. Of course the crew knew nothing of the problems in ditching the Mk XIV, at least not from us.

With a lot of fuel gone I managed to gain another fifty feet without needing too much power. The problems of overheating the good engines and trying to keep the aircraft on course while climbing could not be ignored, nor overcome all that easily.

Our position had to be transmitted every twenty minutes. Apart from strictly pertinent remarks, no one spoke. After well over two hours' flying we reached St Eval, the nearest aerodrome, where the aircraft had to be towed away after we had landed.

The next flight was again towards the Channel Islands. That night I was not able to rid myself of excessive fear in order to achieve the fine balance between fear and exhilaration. My reactions were too fast and exaggerated. My hands would sweat every time I had to turn the aircraft towards yet another run past the Islands. The ten and a half hour flight was hell, absolutely endless.

When we returned I was too exhausted to face the delicious egg, bacon and chips. In time-honoured fashion I divided it among the crew, then drank coffee and smoked cigarettes.

Two days later, just when I was due for leave, I was called in by the squadron adjutant. I was to report to the Air Ministry in London the next day. No reason was given.

The first person I met inside the building was Geniek. We looked at one another. We knew instantly why we were here. Somebody had 'shopped' us.

Geniek was extremely concerned. He was at present at the fighter OTU near Whitchurch, flying Spitfires. Not unnaturally he was worried in case we were suspended from flying.

A few minutes later we were called into separate offices. An NCO sat at one desk, a typewriter in front of him. An officer sat at a desk facing me.

'Your name?'

'Eugeniusz Jaworski.'

The officer exchanged a glance with the NCO, who left the room.

'Look, we know everything. So let's not waste time. It'll only make things more difficult for you.'

I had a momentary urge to say nothing. This might be MI5 or whatever, but their opening lines were not very impressive. Were they bluffing?

'Can I see my friend first?'

'Certainly.'

Geniek looked distinctly unhappy, and I suddenly felt sick.

'They know everything,' he said, resignedly.

I went back into the office.

'My real name is Josef Jaworzyn . . .' I began. The typewriter clacked away. About an hour later I signed the statement. I was then taken to Geniek's office in a deflated mood. We were left alone for a time, but we sat in silence, emotionally spent. What now?

At last the door opened, and what looked like a crowd of officers and NCOs poured in. There were two colonels among them, one of whom was my former squadron commander, then a wing commander, now a group captain. Seeing me, he shook his head in disbelief. I fancied that once again there was a twinkle in his eyes.

'Come on then, Geniek, or Josef, whoever is who . . . Let's hear the whole story again.'

Silence fell while Geniek told his story. When my turn came

167

Korbut waved his hand.

'I don't want to hear anything from you. You've got a penchant for getting yourself into dramatic situations. I can vouch for that, if nothing else.'

Next day, instead of going on leave we were sent back to our respective units. Our identity cards were confiscated; temporary cards would be issued to us in our units. That alone confined us to camp, since there was no way out without conventional ID.

I had a few bad days, with the crew on leave and everyone in the squadron knowing. Their reactions ranged widely, often not very favourably, as I was to find out. However, I had no time to be concerned with the opinions of others.

On the third day after my return from London I was called into the squadron commander's office.

The adjutant saw me.

'The Wingco's been called away urgently,' he said. 'Sit down, have a cigarette.'

I did not like the look on his face. He turned away from me.

'What's wrong?'

'I don't know . . .'

'Well?'

'Your friend, Geniek, I'm afraid he's dead, killed in an air crash.'

'God.'

In silence he passed a telegram to me. 'Please inform Mr E. Jaworski, believed to be on your squadron, that his friend Sgt Josef Jaworzyn lost his life yesterday, Thursday 27th April 1944, as the result of an aircraft accident.'

'I'm terribly sorry,' he mumbled. 'You can have leave to go there of course. I'll get a travel warrant for you as quickly as I can, but everything is in such a mess, what with your name changes, and now Geniek . . .' His voice tailed off.

Next morning I was on my way to Whitchurch, a long and complex journey from Barnstaple. I arrived at the RAF station late in the afternoon and reported to the adjutant.

'So you're the real Jaworzyn. I'm terribly sorry about your friend. Most unfortunate, you've missed the ceremony.'

'What ceremony?'

'Didn't you know?' Your friend was on a practice formation flight at 9,000 feet when another Spitfire collided with his aircraft and cut its whole tail off. He dived into the ground a few miles from here. It's moorland there, boggy. People dug very deep but had to give up in the end. Our padre went there this morning to say mass. We'll put a grave stone there, of course.' He shrugged, and busied himself with his papers.

'Can I have a travel warrant back to Chivenor, please?'

'Tonight?'

'Yes, please.'

'As you wish.'

My spirit could not have sunk lower during the whole of the war. The one death that was not like any other since the war had started had occurred now.

With some others, ingredients such as fear mixed with an immediately suppressed pleasure of being alive were the dominant emotions. With Geniek, things were different. This was so personal, and my grief was pure and simple.

Sitting by myself in an empty compartment of the midnight train, tears streamed down my face. I tried to recall Geniek's face just before our last parting, failed, then remembered him on the many other occasions that made up the many facets of our relationship. I was the more affected because only then did I realise that the expected immunity from the final disaster which I, as an individual, always had in mind I had also automatically extended to Geniek also.

CHAPTER TWELVE

Northern Approaches

I had a rather washed out feeling over the next few days, and I was therefore not particularly stirred up by the news that the squadron was moving.

Apparently the U-boats were no longer a menace in terms of their numbers or ability to surface at will. The few which made for the French harbours now were equipped with a good radar and a schnorkel, an arrangement of pipes and tubes which allowed the U-boats to stay under water while driven by their diesel engines. Also, by then Coastal Command had enough aircraft to patrol the Bay of Biscay. They did still require aircraft to reinforce the blockade of the northern seas against submarines, and our destination was a far cry from Chivenor. It was RAF Benbecula, located in the Outer Hebrides.

It took three hours of flying to reach our new base. As we were circling over Benbecula we saw that the contrast between North Devon in summer and here was going to make it tricky for us to adapt. The islands were all but devoid of green fields, trees were nowhere to be found. Lakes and bare rocks did not just dominate but were the landscape. This did not look like an easy place to fly from. The Swordfish pilots whom we were relieving put the finishing touches to strapping their bikes to the aircraft fuselages. They were heading for more favourable climes now, and looked at us sardonically.

Within days of our arrival the gales began to blow. On one occasion we watched a civilian De Havilland Dove land. It touched the runway on full power while the waiting ground crew took hold of the wing tips and held on until the aircraft unloaded its cargo. Then they let it go, and the plane was instantly in the air.

As our station was not ready to fly us out, we were sent to Tiree for our first operations. My first experience of flying from Tiree was not a spectacular one. The night was dark and stormy, the take-off rather tricky. But not as tricky as it was ten minutes later when we had an engine failure. With the full operational overload still weighing us into unstable flying characteristics I was forced to jettison the bombs and a great deal of petrol also once the engine had failed. We landed safely, but Tiree had no spares for our aircraft. We could not return to base until the following afternoon without even an operation to show.

Our lifestyle at Benbecula soon began to deteriorate. The planners had surpassed themselves in dispersing the living quarters. In gales it was impossible to reach the mess. No road of any kind was laid out to our huts, and the winds were so strong that we could not walk over the crest of hill separating us from the mess. Luckily, a few crofters' cottages close to us kept us supplied with farm produce. Wrobel, our enterprising gunner, once even brought us a chicken. It might still have lived to a ripe old age, for no one wanted to kill it. Then, with the gale not blowing itself out after two or three days, the crew told me that as captain I had a duty to keep them supplied with food. It was therefore forced on me to execute the poor bird. It tasted delicious.

Finally, the administrators, in their great wisdom, installed ropes over the most exposed places, leaving us to struggle in for the meals.

We flew two operational flights in quick succession, and for a variety of reasons the duration of the flights was reduced to nine hours. The total distance we covered remained the same. We flew on northerly patrols, towards the Orkneys, the Shetland Islands and Iceland. The weather was unkind at that time of the year, and the flights often turned out to be chores. The enemy was difficult to find, and in those places where he might be caught the flying conditions required much concentration. The environment was hostile. There were no places to make forced landings here, only rock and water. In the persistently bad weather, low cloud ceiling, any mechanical fault could not be ignored. One had to return straightaway, often cursing the wasted effort of setting out.

The bleak and unfriendly atmosphere of Benbecula depressed many people in the squadron, but it was essential that the pilots adjust as quickly as possible to the very different flying conditions. For those of us who spent all our flying time at low levels, there were basic differences which gave each aerodrome its distinct characteristics. At Benbecula, the weather conditions and high terrain rising directly from the sea dominated our thinking. Under these circumstances, the danger posed by the German fighters and the enemy coast over the horizon were soon forgotten. Instead, the Scottish mountains, looming at heights well above those we flew at, and the constant gales became the focal points for our worries.

The time came for our fourth operation from Benbecula. This time I was to take Tad Kesprowicz to fly with us as co-pilot. He had just arrived at the squadron with a new crew from the OTU. This would be his familiarisation flight, which would give him the feel for the current squadron operational practices.

On the day of the operation, we woke to the sound of the howling wind. Heavy rain beat like bullets on the corrugated iron roof of our 'barrel of fun', as the huts were called. By the time we arrived at the mess, we were soaked to the skin, and not in particularly good moods.

'Don't bother to come with us,' I said to Tad. 'I can't see much chance of our being able to test fly the aircraft.'

He stayed, playing bridge. The rest of us – myself, Wrobel acting as radar operator and gunner, the wireless operator and the navigator – arrived at the dispersal point at eleven a.m.

'You must be joking', said the ground crew chief. He went to the telephone and returned looking subdued. 'Well, we'll start her for you.'

I taxied to the take-off point as skilfully as the wind would allow me to, then took off with the Control's permission.

Immediately the wind seemed to lift us sharply. I could not even reach down to pull up the undercarriage until we came out of the squall. There were many other squalls, each taking the ceiling down to between three hundred and six hundred feet. The visibility decreased to a few hundred yards repeatedly. The sea was grey, with white foam streaks marking out the enormous waves. The western approaches to our rocky islands were almost impassable due to the fury of the sky and sea.

Without the usual operational load, the aircraft rocked and danced in the sky. We did not stay up very long . . . On the landing approach, no one was in a hurry to stay with me in the pilot's cabin, but prudently took positions somewhere back in the fuselage.

I put down no more than 30° flaps, and roared towards the runway, narrowly missing the duty pilot's little hut. Somehow the aircraft managed to stick to the runway, and we arrived back at the dispersal point unscathed. We were back in the mess in time for lunch.

'You did fly then?' asked Tad.

'Yes, yes,' I replied. 'It's not too bad really, just a bit bumpy.'

Wrobel rolled his eyes. I shrugged. It was not a case of heroics, more an attempt to indulge in some wishful thinking for the evening's operational flight.

The evening briefing was not reassuring. There were four crews in attendance. We were to take off at thirty-minute intervals, then spread out over various patrol areas. Ours was the most northerly, moving towards the Faeroe Islands then on to Iceland. The weatherman spread out a chart of deep depressions, looking slightly guilty. Like us, he was not yet used to the new flying conditions. He confined himself to the facts.

'Borderline weather. You might end up being recalled.'

Evening came. The wind blew relentlessly, throwing handfuls of fine rain into our faces while we struggled up the ladder into the aircraft.

The crew was quiet, inclined to low spirits over the coming flight rather than the usual adrenaline-based excitement. This was a far cry from the Bay of Biscay patrols, and no comparison to any weather we had ever experienced in Poland.

The take-off was treacherous, straight into pitch black night. Instantly we were swept into turbulence. At such moments I hated the Wellingtons, and would have given anything for a heavy, four-engined aircraft.

I could hear the navigator swearing with great feeling over the intercom. He was easily airsick, and was obviously starting early. But this sinking, overturning bumping at low speed and no altitude did nothing for me, either. But the aircraft recovered, and there was no time to brood – we had a great deal more of this in store for us.

For a time we flew parallel to the island. I was kept busy, particularly as the magnetic compass was not too reliable up here.

Despite his sickness, the navigator had to work away, continuously monitoring our progress. The engine noise at least was reassuring. In our cockpit the needles on the luminous dials and gauges oscillated wildly in the sharp, violent turbulences. Water streamed through the fine cracks in the windshields, spraying both of us. Tad's face was ashen.

I needed something to distract me from my mind's vision of the wildly swinging wings and the boiling sea below us. The conditions remained terrible, but we could not turn back. We had to wait for the Group to make the first move.

After about an hour, the navigator came on the intercom. 'Wind velocity fifty-five miles per hour.'

I shifted uneasily. By then we had flown clear of the Hebrides, and were well on our way towards the Faeroes.

'Wind velocity sixty miles per hour.'

I stayed silent, battling the aircraft ceaselessly in an attempt to lessen the effect of the increasing gale force wind. I could not ask the Group to recall us.

We changed course towards Iceland. The wind velocity increased, the aircraft was barely controllable. I tried to climb, but even at seven hundred feet we found ourselves in incredibly turbulent cloud.

Three hours passed. Tad and I had not been able to change over. I was still waiting for the Group's recall signal, wondering what the weather was like at the base. At that moment, Wrobel reported a blip on the radar; nine miles, 80° starboard.

I turned on course. The ferocity of the gale had not decreased. The blip disappeared in the sea returns more than a mile away, then reappeared again, I could see nothing below, and the conditions made it dangerous to descend below two hundred feet.

'Navigator, have you got any reports of our shipping in this area?' I asked. The answer was negative.

I made a cautious run over the location of whatever was on the sea. The turbulence threw the aircraft more than a hundred feet up and down. I could see nothing.

'Wireless operator, message to Group,' I said. 'Radar contact in position . . . possible surface vessel. Send instructions.'

We dropped a flare float, which vanished almost at once.

'Message from the Group,' said the wireless operator. 'Return to base at once.'

I had no desire to spend any time wondering about this reply. It was a reprieve, even with the head winds to cope with. It took us more than two hours to reach the base – we had been flying in the storm for more than seven hours in total. I waited anxiously for the weather report from the base, which the wireless operator obtained just twenty minutes before ETA.

'Wind 45, gusting from 240°, cloud base 300 to 700 feet, cloud over 10/10 squalls. Runway in use: 27. Extreme caution on approach.'

No alternative for diversion was given. Realistically, no aerodrome in the vicinity would offer any better conditions, and with the darkness would be even less familiar.

Wrobel led us in until I could see the aerodrome lights, intermittently visible through the spray of the rain and the darkness. At five hundred feet, we were at the base of the clouds. I had as clear a picture in my mind of the aerodrome as I needed in order to land, but I had some difficulty in turning the aircraft into the wind safely. I rushed through the drill, lowering the undercarriage; then, with the engines nearly on full power I made an approach.

'Flaps 15°', I said at last.

The runway danced wildly in front of us, at times seemingly above us. Again I tried to wish myself into a heavy aircraft, but had to face the realities of the situation – if I lost concentration for a second we would be picked up in pieces. We were approaching at a strange angle. I gunned the port engine, used the rudder, and waited for the bump. Finally the bump came, and with the speed down, the aircraft stayed on the ground.

When we reached the dispersal point, there was a sizeable crowd waiting for us. Once the engines were off, we could hear the roar of the wind around us. The Duty Officer and some others came over to us. I was numb with exhaustion, and had trouble lighting a cigarette.

'Good morning, Mr Jaworzyn,' said the Duty Officer, wrapped up in a duffle coat and countless scarves. It was 3.30 a.m. 'You'd better come with me. You can join the rest of the crew later. Radar operator as well, please.'

Apparently the other crews had returned hours earlier. That piece of news would not go down too well with the navigator!

It was still dark by the time we had been questioned about the blip and written up our reports. We trudged through the rain to our hut, cursing the weather and our luck in not having been recalled earlier. We were soaked when we arrived. The rest of the crew were either asleep, or pretending sleep. We wasted no time in joining them.

It was not all gloom and doom though. The strangeness of the northern lands and the sight of the aurora borealis added a romantic element to the anticipation of flying. When I finally went on leave the complexity of travelling almost defied description, but seeing Pauline, still sergeant in Intelligence at a Polish Bomber Command station, was more than compensatory. When I saw her I had just completed my forty-fifth operational flight. Five more and I would be asked to move on. As we discussed this, Pauline examined me, obviously holding back, waiting for me to say more. I was upset, but felt I could not pursue the topic, nor ask her any leading questions. Finally she changed the subject.

(*Left*) J.F.J. posturing in front of a Halifax of Transport Command. (*Right*) Halifax VIIIc landing.

Halifax VIIIc, Transport Command.

(*Right*) J.F.J. in 1945.

In flight in a Warwick of T
port Command.

J.F.J. in late 1945.

I was quite pleased with the area designated for my first operational flight following my return from leave. We were to cover the stretch between Cape Wrath and the approaches to the Orkney Islands using a 'box' patrol technique. A U-boat had been sighted in that area, but subsequent patrols had failed to discover any further traces.

The weather was reasonable, and it was only a short flight to the patrol area. We carried on circling the area, relying on the radar to keep us away from the land mass. We saw nothing but a couple of frigates, and the time passed slowly.

It was nearly 7 a.m. when I turned on to course 180°, towards the Scottish coast.

'Schnorkel,' said the second pilot. 'Starboard, 80°, about two miles, disappearing.'

I turned; the smoke of the diesel engine was just visible. I dived on full power, knowing we were already too late. I dropped the depth charges on the last point of sighting. We watched the explosions ruffle the sea surface, but nothing else happened. I started to climb in order to allow the wireless operator to start the normal procedures. In less than thirty minutes another Wellington took our place – we made one last search of the attack area, then returned to base.

On return I made a run over the base at low level; we could see the aircrew scrambling for cover as the plane roared above them while they made their way to the mess for breakfast.

We received the depth charge pins, inscribed, as mementos, but the attack could only be considered as inconclusive in terms of damage to the U-boat.

I started thinking about what should happen next. There were now only four more operations left to fly. My strongest inclination was towards the Special Duties Squadron. They had suffered very heavy losses during the Warsaw uprising, and now needed new but experienced crews with at least one operational tour behind them.

In my mind I had jumped the gun as far as completing the tour was concerned. In the next operation we experienced the most difficult weather conditions that we had ever come across.

177

It was fearful. Included in the programme were a force ten gale, heavy rain and hail, and being struck by lightning for the second time.

I gather that being struck twice is a statistical improbability, but it certainly was a reality to us. The build up of the charge on the aircraft seemed very swift this time, but that may have been due to the fact that the extremely heavy disturbances kept me busy and preoccupied with controlling the aircraft. But once again the whole external structure glowed, and the lightning was almost instantly discharged. We all saw a ball of glowing light rushing past my seat down into the fuselage, leaving a trail of destruction behind it.

This time there was damage to the aircraft and to the radio set. We were forced to abandon the operation and return to base without the completion of the patrol.

At last came my final flight. I went out as a senior pilot with a new crew on their first operation rather than with my own crew. We returned on a clear morning after ten and a half hours flying over the Atlantic. On the way back we had met with stronger winds than the navigator had allowed for, and were consequently one and a half hours behind schedule. I was more than not amused; I was anxious: watching the white-capped swell lined up with the strong winds and checking the patrol gauges kept me tense until the last few minutes. I landed the aircraft with a distinct feeling of relief. Enough was enough for Coastal Command. Now for a month on leave in Blackpool, then off to fly the Liberators in Italy.

'Hmmm,' said the Wing Commander, when I reported to him the next morning. 'It's not quite like that, I'm afraid. You're due to start on the next course at the OCTU in ten days' time. So, there's not much point in sending you to Blackpool. The OCTU is in Scotland, anyway.' He paused, and pretended to muse over the problem. 'I tell you what, you can make yourself useful here. You can instruct the new pilots in flying practice until it's time for you to go.'

CHAPTER THIRTEEN
Training Again

Travelling to Crieff on a dull morning in November 1944, I could not help but reflect on how late in the day it was to be trained as an officer. As it was it had taken the Poles more than two years even to decide to set up an approach to the problem. We had too many pre-war officers, the forces were top heavy, and then all the pre-war cadet officers had to be promoted first . . . When it had been finally agreed upon the aircrew still had to be seconded to the Army for over five months; equally disagreeable was the insistence on reverting to the Polish ranks, which meant that a warrant officer might have to stay at the rank of corporal for the duration. Not surprising therefore that the first courses brought in some people who were not really of the same mind as those who had pressed for the OCTU to be opened.

As I travelled, I was not particularly looking forward to the experience. Five months away from flying was not what I had originally envisaged. In retrospect, being sent there was common sense on the part of the squadron CO. I needed to be taken off flying. I was nervous, and my judgements in the air were suffering. My health was not very good either. I smoked a lot, drank, ate little.

The previous winter I had suffered for a period of three to four months with a 'heavy chest cold', which produced bouts of coughing that left me gasping for breath. I do not recall seeing a doctor, nor anyone suggesting that I should. A long time later I learned that this was almost certainly a touch of TB. When the spring came the coughing subsided, and I thought nothing of it until much later.

As I had been told, the Polish Army in Britain, the bulk of which was stationed in Scotland, had retained a rather romantic view of the Air Force which to some extent was a residue of the pre-war attitude. Even now, after three or four courses attended mainly by aircrew they did not seem disillusioned.

I was greeted at the railway station by the NCO in charge, and copiously saluted in the process. Rather taken aback, it took me two days before I could accept that a different point of view from that of my own crew might exist.

But the Army was serious-minded. Officer cadets in the Army had always enjoyed certain privileges. We were therefore treated with respect, but in exchange were expected to respect the rules which had been set out for the running of the OCTU.

At Crieff, while scanning the faces of the aircrew and comparing notes, I took a first count of the casualties suffered by my flying contemporaries. I could check out the Polish students only. Of the thirty-three who had received pilots' wings with me at South Cerney no more than five were still alive. Not much later I was to discover that the number was actually three. Out of thirty-three. Each of these pilots had a crew, which made the toll rise further.

Among the Army personnel I found a few colleagues from schooldays. I learned that a close friend from that time, a German, had joined the Luftwaffe as a pilot, and had lost his life over the Bay of Biscay.

The Army set out to train us in the basics of military discipline as well as to instruct us in fighting in armoured warfare. There were no savage NCOs nor snide officers in evidence. We began by learning how to fight against, and in, tanks and other armoured vehicles. Some of the scenes in the training were quite memorable, and some appeared slightly unreal to us. We enjoyed ourselves a great deal.

In my first lesson in tank driving the instructor refused to be too specific.

'Nothing to it,' he told me. 'After flying an aircraft, it's a piece of cake.'

Ten minutes later I was careering across a very rough Scottish moorland, having enormous difficulty in trying to control and coordinate two steering columns and a clutch, and to see where I was driving through a miniscule gap in the armour in front of me.

When firing the anti-tank Piat I was certain that I caused more harm to myself than I could have done to a tank. One was given a live anti-tank shell and then sent off to a lonely ditch. By then my hands would be so sticky with sweat that I could barely arm the weapon. When I did finally fire, the recoil was so phenomenal that I was bounced back and forth in the narrow trench, my helmet yards away.

After the Piat, the hand grenades were relatively simple. As long as one kept cool. Only the mortar firing caused any problems – especially the six inch monsters, to which we were treated with a demonstration. We sat on a hill top when the characteristic sound of the mortar shell whizzing over one's head suddenly stopped.

'Down, down', shouted the instructors. We threw ourselves into the nearest ditch or any dip in the ground. I lay under three or four highly decorated fighter pilots, all trying to claw deeper into the earth. The shell exploded on the hill top, spraying the area with anti-personnel fragments. We had three wounded, all conscious but bleeding profusely. I think that from then on we gave more detailed attention to the vast range of the Army's weaponry, and their nasty side effects.

While talking to acquaintances in the Army I could not help but be struck by their shining, idealistic patriotism, their absolute commitment to their obligations and duties as Poles. At times I was touched by such anachronistic attitudes, at others infuriated. Somehow our lives in the Air Force did not seem to translate themselves into such specific expressions of our nationalism.

About that time it was announced that I had been awarded the Cross of Valour, and within a week or two the Bar for the Cross also. The timing was to prove to be of significance from my point of view. If I was to have any benefit for having the decorations, the Army saw to it that I did there and then. I was suitably flattered by their attention. Nevertheless, I was keenly aware that such decorations were part of yesterday's achievements; it would have been a mistake to use the occasion as a guide as to what might happen tomorrow.

However, I am certain that the period at the OCTU had done a great deal for many of the aircrew – we had recovered a great amount of our emotional and physical health.

Exercises over, we spent much of the time in an excellent canteen serviced by the FANY girls. Highly intelligent and enormously patient, the girls were good companions and the most appropriate link with the British community at large. For the Poles, and the Army in particular, early 1945 further deepened their unease about the future. The separation of the British people's view of the war from that as perceived by the Poles continued. The external forces which began to shape the world – apart from the straightforward progress in the military fight against the Germans – if perceived at all, were of little concern to the British. The tragic death of General Sikorski had exacerbated the 'Polish problem' of the time. The war seemed to be almost over, and the expectation of a good life afterwards was already prevalent. The complications of the Polish situation were by then something of a bore. Little wonder that the FANY girls had a difficult task taking on discussions with the Poles which few of their male compatriots would have been prepared to do. Of course, with the Polish Army present there was much bowing and hand-kissing, and all of the other social graces in which the Army was greatly accomplished. No doubt a lot of the latter compensated for the unpleasantness of the former.

*

Near the end of the course we had a visit from a high-ranking officer who had taken part in the Warsaw uprising. The little he was able to tell us struck terror into our hearts. Since then, the horrendous story of the massacre of nearly 300,000 Polish civilians and the systematic destruction of over 90% of the city by specially selected troops of the German Army has been told

many times. But the emotions of the Poles in Britain who heard
of the struggle are hard to describe. The feelings of helplessness
and frustration were turned greatly towards the West; the Western countries were seen as selfish, cold and calculating, and
once again failed to face up to the scale of the atrocities being
committed in occupied Europe. There were no counter-
measures against the 'Total War', not even a consideration of
them. The powerful Western war machine could but cope with
the conventional strategies. Even the biggest and most massive
weapon of the war – the Air Forces of the West – could only be
handled in a conventional way. After all, the generals fighting
World War II had been trained in World War I.

We returned to marching and counter-marching. We fired
more bullets and threw more hand grenades until the final day
came. The passing out parade included top brass from London.
This was also the day when decorations awarded previously
were presented.

The parade was but a formality. By then there were no more
commissions for Polish aircrew. I do not recall any fuss being
made over the subject, either by me or anyone else on the course.
By then I was ready and keen to leave the cold climate of Scotland
for the 'real' life of flying.

However, I found that I had been under a misapprehension
on a more weighty matter than the commission. The Special
Squadron which I was to join no longer flew operations over
Europe. By early 1945 such flights were fraught with political
problems. It would not have been wise to send Poles on such
missions from Britain or anywhere else. The continent of Europe
was rapidly polarising into separate political camps, and sending
Polish aircrew could further complicate local problems. The
squadron was therefore transferred to Transport Command.

*

Spring 1945. The RAF station I was travelling to was RAF Chedburgh near Bury St Edmunds. I had hoped to fly the special mission Halifaxes, but that had been months ago. During the war it

183

might as well have been years back.

I was not surprised therefore to find that the squadron was converting to Warwicks and modified Halifaxes, which had been adapted for flying with Transport Command. Another novelty awaited me; the station was run almost entirely by Poles, but with a few English personnel in the administration. Pauline was also there, which provided a bright spot.

The aircrew were highly experienced. Everyone had at least one operational tour behind him. There was a great deal of re-training involved here, since the crew for the Warwicks consisted of a pilot, navigator and wireless operator only, while the Halifax required two pilots, an engineer, a wireless operator and optionally a navigator and a dispatcher. I found out that our main tasks would include bringing troops back home from the Middle East for demobilisation, and taking supplies to the Far East in the Halifaxes.

The atmosphere was very different from that of an operational squadron, not only for the obvious reason of not flying high risk missions, but because once again the underlying worries pressed hard on the Poles.

The European war was coming to an end. The German Army, who for years had been unbeatable by any army of a single nation, was now being crushed under mountains of equipment, unprecedented fire power and the homicidal mistakes of Hitler. There were no miracles left for the Germans. But at that moment they continued to fight, and many people were still to die.

Already the emerging Europe was much changed from the pre-war years. For the Poles, the future looked very uncertain, and here in the squadron the diminished commitments to the flying duties opened up a period of speculation and discussions.

However, as far as I was concerned I was back to flying. The adrenaline poured, the excitement of flying was with me again. I was quickly immersed in the technical discussions of the new air-craft, the flying problems. The roar of the engines, the night fly-ing . . . We were back in action. I was aware of the political discussions taking place, but took no part in them.

I found no problems in flying the Warwicks, probably because they came from the same stable as the Wellingtons. But their Pratt and Whitney engines were not entirely compatible with the aircraft. A spate of engine trouble descended upon us, and this reduced the level of the political arguments. The engines were liable to dramatic backfiring while being started, which in turn could result in internal fires. In addition, a deficiency in the fuel system design could on occasions lead to the fuel flow to the engines being reduced during flight. Sudden engine failure followed. I had a crew which by then included a flight engineer, but this did not prevent us from falling victim to an engine failure followed by a rather embarrassing sequence of events.

We had set off at midnight on a long flight, the first leg of which led from East Anglia to the Scilly Islands, then north-east to York. A series of such flights were required to qualify for the Transport Command duties.

After just over an hour of uneventful flying, the port engine suddenly wheezed, coughed and expired; red lights on the fuel pressure gauges suggested the reason but indicated no cure. As the other engine would fail within minutes, I called Mayday as the regulations required of me. An aerodrome answered immediately, very close, just under us. We had reached the Devon/Cornwall border. I saw the aerodrome lights come on while the aircraft was in a steep turn without power. Judging by the number and the nature of the lights the aerodrome was a small one. I used the gliding path very carefully, made certain of touching down at the very beginning of the flarepath and applied the brakes as soon as was practicable. And so in less than five minutes after we had been droning peacefully, settled into a long round-Britain flight, we were down on the ground, on an obscure airfield.

The next day I saw that I was right. The aerodrome was a tiny grass satellite of an SFTS, sitting on top of a hill. The base informed me that they were sending another aircraft with the mechanics. I was not happy. To a pilot coming in in daytime, not in an emergency, the landing ground would look no bigger than the flight deck of an aircraft carrier. Now in a Warwick . . . My fears were justified. A rather less experienced pilot brought six mechanics, was unable to stop in time, and damaged the under-carriage. Immediately the weather closed down.

We poked about gloomily. At long last, with my aircraft repaired, I was told to fly back to base with fourteen people on board. As I taxied to the take-off point I glanced at the field. A dip in the middle made it look absurdly short, and its abrupt disappearance over the edge was unnerving. This might have been all right for Tiger Moths or Miles Masters . . .

I managed the take-off, but to my horror had to return the next day in an Oxford to bring back parts for the other Warwick. The idea was that of the squadron commander, who was far from sympathetic concerning my forced landing.

'I don't know how the hell you managed to get in and out of there,' he said, 'but . . .'

So, having landed in the Oxford I was left to wait for the mechanics to finish the repairs then take the aircraft back to base. The next night we were off on the cross-country flight again, and completed it after six hours' flying.

One evening I saw a small crowd in front of the DRO board. There was a list of the latest decorations. Together with another pilot, I received the Virtuti Militari, the highest Polish Military decoration. By then both the number of people receiving it and those who had received it and were still alive was decreasing in a logarithmic decay order.

I read and reread the DRO. Then I glanced at the faces of the aircrew around me. Curiosity and pleasure at seeing one of their own members being awarded the decoration. Others looked unhappy, even grim. I walked away quickly. There would be lots of time for celebration and for arguments.

Did I really deserve to be awarded the Virtuti Militari? Once again I went over my flying career and background: at some stage I had been one of the youngest pilots serving during the war in the RAF. The medical board probably had it wrong about the bad heart, but at one point I had certainly flown quite a number of flights with active TB. Perhaps I had pressed on with operations which many others would have abandoned. I reflected that this latter made for few friends amongst one's own crew. But did this and other factors amount to that special effort expected under the circumstances? Some people thought so. After all, even a squadron commander could only make a recommendation. It was up to a committee in London to make the decision.

I did reflect that had I been in an RAF unit at the time of the discovery of the name change with Geniek, I would almost certainly have ended up in prison. Law and order would have come to the fore. There might have been some mitigating circumstances, which would possibly have led to a reduction of the sentence. Perhaps.

In the pre-war days I had first heard of the pomp and circumstances, the privileges which the decoration entitled one to. But that was long ago.

Within a few weeks we had a visit from a Polish General. The whole station paraded, the two of us at the head of the line of those receiving decorations. Then we stood on the stand with the General to receive the salute. Afterwards, we put the decorations well away . . .

At about the same time, the squadron began to take in more crews. Most of the pilots had already flown four engine aircraft such as Liberators or Lancasters. I was now put on a list of Transport Command Halifax pilots. In due course I would start a conversion course for these planes.

CHAPTER FOURTEEN

Epilogue

We now reached the time when the last battles of the war were being fought in Europe. My training continued to progress satisfactorily. I had mastered the flying of the troop-carrying Warwick, and was preparing for flying to Europe. France, Italy and Greece were initially to be the countries of our flights. While the plans for the operation of the unit were being finalised, I volunteered with the crew for a short-term secondment to an RAF Ferry Unit. Apparently the RAF wanted to replace its obsolescent Wellingtons in Egypt with the new Mk V Warwicks.

Together with a few other crews we went to the RAF station in South Devon. At once I knew that this had been a mistake. This was the RAF of non-operational units, and the urgency of the war was disappearing rapidly in many of the other British units. The ground crew were no longer interested. I watched, puzzled and anxious as they took an interminable time to service the aircraft – badly. The situation was now one in which one had to make continuous judgements in which faults in the aircraft would have to be tolerated, if one wanted to fly at all with the risks involved. Every repair meant long delays.

If this was unpleasant, it was understandable. Additional problems accumulated. As we marched smartly around the station, saluting almost non-stop, my enthusiasm for that trip to Egypt began to wane. So did that of my crew. However, our minds were made up for us. Assigned to a flight commanded by a tall, slim red-haired squadron leader AFC, I ran into instant trouble.

At the first parade I was assigned to fly as a second pilot to Malta, with an English sergeant whose total flying time was 162 hours.

I said, 'Sorry, sir, there must be some mistake.'

A silence fell on the crew room. The squadron leader glared at me.

'Aircrew dismissed. Mr Jaworzyn to stay behind.'

The room cleared rather quickly.

'You are disobeying a direct order, Mr Jaworzyn', he said icily.

'I am not, sir. I volunteered to fly an aircraft, and not to be a second pilot. The sergeant is a trainee on a difficult flight, in an aircraft without dual controls.'

'You're suspended.'

'Yes, sir.'

The next day I was back at Chedburgh. Dejectedly, I reflected that this was the RAF at its worst, all rank pulling and discipline, and no performance. Later on I could not be certain whether this incident did not bear on my behaviour during the crisis which was about to descend on me. Immediately after my return I recounted what had happened to a group of aircrew. Nobody made any comment. To most of them, this was just a confirmation of the opinions which they had already formed, or situations they had themselves encountered at RAF stations. The changing attitude towards flying in general within the RAF was all too apparent. To the Poles it was not really news, merely a manifestation of the phenomenon of the time.

Pauline was glad to see me back. I did not tell her all. I did realise that a new factor had entered into our relationship and was interfering with it. With a horrific sense of loss, I realised that our relationship was coming to an end. Pauline wanted me, but she wanted something else besides, perhaps an understanding on my part, an appreciation of the changing times, a commitment to accept the change.

I could not, or would not change. I watched with grief as her friends closed in around her. They were all officers, which by itself had meant nothing until now. After all, we had known each other for a long time, particularly for a wartime relationship. But now everything was changing. One way or another, I would have to fit in with the change.

Early in the Spring I flew to the Middle East. When I finally made it back after a long wait in Malta for an aircraft, Pauline was gone. She was on leave, pending commission, followed by an immediate posting. I knew where she went, of course. I did nothing, and we never met again.

*

The Poles were becoming gloomy. Even the aircrew were losing their ebullience. With German resistance coming to an end, the time was inevitably approaching for momentous decisions. Except for the defeat of the Germans, at the end of the war nothing was happening the way people had thought it would.

May 7th 1945: The aerodrome was silent. This was VE Day. At breakfast time we shuffled around listlessly, glanced at the newspapers, kept the radio switched off.

After breakfast I went back to my living quarters. I busied myself with making a fire in our iron stove, not really caring whether we needed one or not. Mechanically, I cleaned out the stove, packed it, lit it, and then sat down in front of it, absent-mindedly poking at the ashes.

Could the war really have finished? On this historic day, the first day of peace in Europe, I could have looked back over the last five and a half years, could have reflected on the topics which had vitally related to me during the period of the war.

I could have thought about the Poles in the West, and how their resistance to change which had irritated me so much over the past few years was but one facet of being a Pole, of the survival of Poland in the face of pressure by invading and hostile nations. I could have thought of Poland, of my family and what their feelings might be at this time.

I could have thought of flying, and the frightful price it had extracted in the lives of most of my friends. And of the vast and relentless sea over which I, a man of the mountains, had spent so much of my time flying, and over which I had experienced so many emotions.

Of the mystery of Wacek's disappearance. And of Aniela whom I was never to hear of again. And of Pauline. And of many others, and a multitude of other facets of the war which had affected me one way or another.

Perhaps I did try to think of at least some of these subjects. But as I stared disconsolately at the fire I certainly let my thoughts return to flying and to the Warwicks. It would be perhaps two days before things would be back to normal. So, in say, three days' time we should be able to test the aircraft, and weather permitting should be off to Greece by the weekend.

I lit another cigarette. I began to look further ahead. Like flying to the Far East in the brand new Halifaxes . . .

APPENDICES

APPENDIX 1

Polish Air Force in Great Britain in World War II

A total of 16 operational squadrons and a range of supporting units formed the core of the Polish Air Force in Great Britain.

The following were involved:

No 300 Squadron (Bomber) stationed primarily at RAF Hemswell.

No 301 Squadron (Bomber) stationed at Swinderby, Hemswell, then as a flight of 138 Special Duties Squadron Tempsford, Sidi Amor, Brindisi, and finally at RAF Chedburgh.

No 302 Squadron (Fighter) stationed at Duxford and numerous other stations in Britain and on the Continent.

No 303 Squadron (Fighter)

No 304 Squadron (Bomber and Coastal Command)

No 305 Squadron (Bomber) stationed at RAF Bramcote, Seyrston, Lindholm, Hemswell and other locations.

No 306 Squadron (Fighter) stationed at Church Fenton, Northolt, Speke, Heston and other locations.

No 307 Squadron (Night Fighter) stationed at Squire's Gate, Colerne, Exeter, Fairwood Common, Predannack, Drem, Church Fenton and others.

No 308 Squadron (Fighter) stationed at Northolt, Church Fenton, Heston and other (27) RAF aerodromes.

No 309 Squadron (Army Cooperation, Reconnaisance-Fighter and Fighter) stationed at Renfrew, Crail, Gatwick and others.

No 315 Squadron (Fighter) stationed at Acklington, Northolt, Andrews Field and others.

No 316 Squadron (Fighter) stationed at Pembrey, Colerne, Church Tauton, Northolt, West Malling and others.

No 317 Squadron (Fighter) stationed at Acklington, Northolt, Heston and others.

No 318 Squadron (Fighter and Reconnaissance) stationed at

RAF Detling then in Egypt and Italy.
No 663 Squadron (Air Operational) stationed in Italy.

Training Units included the following:
IETS at Blackpool.
Air Crew Training Centre at Hucknall.
Polish Flights at:
No 58 Fighter OTU at Grangemouth, then Rednall.
No 18 Bomber OTU at Bramcote.
No 6 (Coastal Command) OTU at RAF Silloth.
No 25 EFTS at Hucknall.
No 15 SFTS at Newton.

Maintenance Units included the following:
No 71 MU at Slough.
No 58 MU at Newark.
No 408 ASP (Air Stores Park)
No 411 RSU (Repair and Salvage Unit)
No 72 MTLRU (Motor Transport Light Repair Unit)
No 5029 ACS (Airfield Construction Squadron)

There was a Polish Flight with No 945 Balloon Unit, eventually named Polish Balloon Unit.

Polish pilots flew with the Atlantic Ferry Organisation, the RAF Delivery Unit in Africa, and in the Polish Air Force Unit, RAF Middle East.

A Polish Flight was formed with No 112 Squadron which flew Hurricanes in Libya. This flight was eventually disbanded due to the lack of trained Polish pilots to replace those lost in the squadron.

There were 8,154 Polish airmen in Britain in October 1940, and 14,351 in May 1945. By 1945 the Polish aircrew losses totalled 2,416 killed, missing or POW.

APPENDIX 2

304 (Polish) Squadron

22.9.1940   Officially formed at RAF Station Bramcote
1.12.1940   Moved to RAF Seyrston (Notts)
20.7.1941   Moved to RAF Lindholm (Yorks)
10.5.1942   Moved to RAF Tiree (Scotland): to No 15 Coastal
             Command Group
13.6.1942   RAF Dale (South Wales): to No 19 Coastal
             Command Group
30.3.1943   RAF Docking (Norfolk)
10.6.1943   RAF Davidstow Moor (Cornwall)
20.12.1943   RAF Predannack (Cornwall)
19.3.1944   RAF Chivenor (Devon)
19.9.1944   RAF Benbecula (Outer Hebrides)
5.3.1945   RAF St Eval (Cornwall)
5.9.1945   RAF Chedburgh (Suffolk): Transport Command
September 1946. The squadron is disbanded.
Losses in Bomber and Coastal Commands: 243 aircrew killed,
46 aircraft lost.

APPENDIX 3

Radar in Coastal Command

ASV: Air to Surface Vessel. Operated on 176 MHz on Mk XIII Wellington. 'Stickleback' ASV aerials on top of the fuselage. Range up to twelve miles on surface craft in quiet seas. Limits of resolution – approx. one and a half miles because of 'sea returns'.

10cm. ASV radar: 'chin' under the nose of the aircraft contained the scanner. First installed in twelve Wellingtons stationed at RAF Chivenor.

Leigh Light: Long history of delays against development problems, opposition and indifference. Power: 22 million candle power light with a 10° flat-topped beam. Located in a retractable turret, operated from the aircraft nose. Special attack technique was developed by No 172 Squadron flying from Chivenor, using Wellington Mk VIII and ASV Mk II. First attack 5th July 1942.

GLOSSARY

U/T	Under training
IFTS	Initial Flying Training School
EFTS	Elementary Flying Training School
SFTS	Service Flying Training School
OA	Call sign for attack by enemy fighters
OCTU	Officer Cadet Training Unit
OTU	Operational Training Unit
AFU	Advanced Flying Unit
PO	Pilot Officer
W/Op	Wireless Operator
DRO	Daily Routine Orders
RDF	Radio Direction Finding
IFF	Identification, Friend or Foe
ETA	Estimated Time of Arrival
ASV	Air to Surface Vessel
FIDO	Fog Investigation and Dispersal Operation

INDEX

Index

Anglesey, 64.
Anson, Avro, 60, 61.
Antoniewicz, Leopold, 153, 154.
ASV (Air to Surface Vessel), 90, 91.
Auschwitz, 18, 56.

Barnstaple, 128, 133, 137, 156, 164, 168.
Battle of the Atlantic, 67, 69, 128.
Battle of Britain, 15, 23.
Bay of Biscay, 69, 71, 74, 76, 77, 78, 89, 90, 92, 93, 94, 102, 109, 110, 111, 125, 129, 143, 148, 150, 158, 170, 173, 180.
Beaufighter, Bristol, 60, 61, 76, 78.
Beaufort, Bristol, 60, 69.
Benbecula, RAF, 170, 171, 172.
Blackpool, 15, 16, 17, 19, 20, 22, 25, 39, 49, 50, 60, 65, 79, 80, 107, 109, 121, 137, 178.
Blenheim, Bristol, 23.
Bomber Command, 50, 51, 56, 65, 67, 69, 72, 73, 81, 82, 83, 84, 90, 100, 111, 117, 136, 176.
Bordeaux, 84, 86, 87.
Boscombe Down, RAF, 153.
Botha, Blackburn, 52, 53, 57, 62, 65, 73.
Brest, 74, 75, 90, 96, 103.
Bristol, 37, 38.
Bury St Edmunds, 183.

Cape Wrath, 177.
Carlisle, 25, 28, 29, 33, 37, 42, 43.
Chartershall, RAF, 60.

Chedburgh, RAF, 183, 191.
Chivenor, RAF, 128, 130, 149, 155, 169.
Churchill, Winston S., 50.
Cieszyn, 20.
Cirencester, 39.
Coastal Command, 56, 60, 67, 68, 72, 73, 79, 81, 91, 92, 100, 124, 128, 143, 153, 178.
Cologne, 56.
Crieff, RAF, 179, 180.
Cross of Valour (Polish), 80, 181.
Czekelski, Wacek, 72, 74–80, 83–99, 101, 102, 106, 126, 127, 136, 164, 193.

D-Day, 153, 155, 159.
DFM (Distinguished Flying Medal), 133.
Dale, RAF, 67, 70.
Davidstow Moor, RAF, 82, 89, 97, 130.
Dieppe, 81.
Dinard, 11.
Docking, RAF, 72, 79.
Dove, De Havilland, 170.
Drem System, 151.
Dunkirk, 11.

Exeter, 88, 89.
Exmouth, 89.

Faeroe Islands, 173, 174.
Fastnet, 74.
Ferry Command, 54.

FIDO (Fog Investigation and Dispersal Operation), 132, 133.
Finisterre, 137.
Focke-Wulf, 85, 188.
Frith, J.R., 35, 40–45.
Frylinski, Zyg, 150–153.

Gee box, 100, 102.
Glasgow, 11.
Gloucester, 45.
Gmiter, Kres, 25–31, 33–35, 37, 46–48, 63.
Grantham, RAF, 107, 143.

Hajnowka, 20.
Halifax, Handley Page, 183, 184, 187, 195.
Hemswell, RAF, 21, 56, 65.
Heydrich, Reinhard, 40.
Himmler, Heinrich, 40.
Hitler, Adolf, 184.

Isle of Man, 61.

Jaworski, Eugeniusz ('Geniek'), 12, 13, 16, 17, 19, 20, 21, 24, 32, 33, 39, 56, 65, 66, 79, 80, 81, 107, 123, 143, 167, 168, 169, 187.
Jaworski, K., 60.
Junkers Ju88, 70, 71, 74, 76, 90, 109, 110, 113–116, 130, 156.

Katyn massacre, 98.
Kawa, M., 127, 131–133.
Kesprowitz, Tad, 172–174.
Kieltyka, A., 99, 158.
Korbut, Czeslaw, 95, 96, 102–106, 125, 127, 131, 155, 168.

Ladro, Emil, 109–118, 120, 121.
Lancaster, Avro, 187.
Land's End, 92.
Lawrence, T.E., 50.
Leeds, 121.
Leigh Light, 100, 134, 135, 142, 149, 151, 158.
Liberator, Consolidated, 61, 149, 178, 187.

Lidice, 40.
London, 33, 81, 82, 109, 121, 162, 183.
Lysander, Westland, 52, 53, 57, 59.

Magister, Miles, 26, 27, 30, 31, 43.
The Major – see Stanczuk, E.
Master, Miles, 107, 143, 186.
Messerschmitt Me109, 74, 76, 85, 95.
Messerschmitt Me110, 70, 76, 133.
Miedzybrodski, Leszek, 149–153.
Military Medal (English), 80.
Monte Cassino, 141.
Morpeth, 55, 56, 57.
Morpeth, RAF, 51, 56, 62, 64, 65, 82.
Mosquito, De Havilland, 60, 61, 107.
Moszoro, Wartan, 51 55, 62, 65, 107, 130.
Myszkowski, ('Myszko'), 51, 53.

Newark (Polish Training School), 25.
Newcastle, 51, 52, 57, 64.
Newton, RAF, 34.
Nikel, Frank, 109, 118, 119, 121, 126, 131, 132, 157, 164, 165.
Northolt, RAF, 23–26.

Ochalski, J., 128–130, 156.
Orkney Islands, 171, 177.
Outer Hebrides, 170, 174.
Oxford, Airspeed, 34, 35, 37, 42, 44, 48, 186.

Piserski, Wlad, 111–117.
Plymouth, 89.
Predannack, RAF, 74, 97, 99, 102, 103, 117, 124, 130, 149.
Preston, 14, 16, 19.

Rommel, Erwin, 50.
Ruhr Dam, 82.
Rysko, Rysiek, 38, 49, 51, 53, 62, 63.

St Eval, RAF, 166.
St Jean de Luz, 11.
Scilly Islands, 74, 76, 77, 78, 88, 97, 103, 131, 135, 141, 185.
Shetland Islands, 171.
Sikorski, General Wladyslaw, 182.
Silesia, 69.
Silloth, RAF, 109, 117, 120, 132, 150.
South Cerney, RAF, 34, 60, 180.
Spitfire, Supermarine, 24, 34, 43, 58, 61, 167, 169.
Squires Gates,RAF, 60, 62.
Stanczuk, E. ('The Major'), 72, 77, 84–90, 95, 126, 127.
Steel, Sgt., 47.
Stirling, Short, 23.
Sunderland, Short, 61, 77, 87.
Swordfish, Fairey, 170.

Targowski, Stan, 110, 111.
Tiger Moth, De Havilland, 24, 26, 112, 186.
Tiree, RAF, 56, 171.
Training Command, 60.
Transport Command, 183, 184, 185, 187.
Typhoon, Hawker, 57.

Valley, RAF, 132, 133.

Virtuti Militari, 54, 64, 186.

Wacek – see Czekelski, W.
Warsaw, 81, 165, 177, 182.
Wartan – see Moszoro, W.
Warwick, Vickers-Armstrong, 184, 185, 186, 190, 193.
Weeton, RAF, 14, 15.
Wellington, Vickers, 65, 70, 73, 76, 82, 118, 149, 174, 177, 185, 190.
Wellington, Vickers Mk Ic, 69, 110–117.
Wellington, Vickers Mk X, 73, 83, 84, 109.
Wellington, Vickers Mk XIII, 82, 83, 89, 90, 91, 100, 109.
Wellington, Vickers Mk XIV, 89, 100, 103, 106, 109, 111, 125, 137, 142, 143, 151, 153, 157, 166.
Whitchurch, 167, 168.
Wito, T., 67, 68, 70, 71, 73, 74, 75, 111.
Wnucki, P., 54, 56, 57, 59, 60, 64, 65.
Woodhouse, H.W., 26, 27, 30, 31, 35.
Wrobeleski ('Wrobel'), 121, 139, 140, 141, 171, 172, 173, 175.

Zurek, Stanislaw, 102, 104–106, 109.